WALK WITH JESUS

A Journey Through the Life of Christ

FRANK BALL

Walk with Jesus
A Journey Through the Life of Christ

By Frank Ball

Roaring Lambs Publishing
18383 Preston Road, Suite 406
Dallas, TX 75252

Phone: 972.380.0123

Email: info@RoaringLambs.org
FBall@RoaringLambs.org

RoaringLambs.org

FrankBall.org

Table of Contents

Seeing the Whole Story —Six Sermons that Really Matter ______ 1

SERMON 1: Light That Darkness Couldn't Overcome _ 7
SERMON 2: Heaven Interrupts the Ordinary ______ 18
SERMON 3: The Voice in the Wilderness ______ 28
SERMON 4: Come and See ______ 37
SERMON 5: Authority Like None Other ______ 47
SERMON 6: From Glory to the Cross ______ 56
From Pulpit to Person: Using Eyewitness as an Evangelism Tool ______ 65

Sermons for Special Occasions ______ 73

1. CHRISTMAS SEASON: The Word Became Flesh__ 75
2. LENT (Six Weeks Before Easter): Prepare the Way _ 81
3. PALM SUNDAY: Crown Him or Crucify Him ____ 87
4. MAUNDY THURSDAY: The Table Before the Cross ______ 93
5. GOOD FRIDAY: Not an Accident ______ 98
6. EASTER SUNDAY: The Stone Was Not the End_ 103
7. ASCENSION SUNDAY: Why Jesus Had to Leave 109
8. PENTECOST: When the Fire Fell ______ 114
9. MISSIONS SUNDAY: Sent with Authority ______ 120
10. COMMUNION EMPHASIS SUNDAY: Remembering What It Cost ______ 126
11. CHRIST THE KING SUNDAY: The Throne Isn't Empty ______ 131

12. GRADUATION SERVICES: Follow Me ______ 136
13. MEMORIAL SERVICE: Death Is Not Final____ 142
14. DISCIPLESHIP SUNDAY: Follow Me________ 147
15. STEWARDSHIP SUNDAY: Faithful with What Is His ________________________________ 153

Study Group Sessons________________________________159

Introductory Session: Why *Eyewitness*? Seeing the Whole Story________________________________ 161
STUDY 1: Preparation and Identity______________ 167
STUDY 2: First Signs & Private Conversations _____ 173
STUDY 3: Authority & Opposition______________ 180
STUDY 4: Kingdom Principles ________________ 187
STUDY 5: Power Over Nature & Death __________ 194
STUDY 6: Growing Opposition & Clear Identity ___ 201
STUDY 7: The Cost of Discipleship _____________ 208
STUDY 8 Lost and Found_____________________ 214
STUDY 9: The King Enters Jerusalem ___________ 221
STUDY 10: Ready or Not ______________________ 228
STUDY 11: The Passion _______________________ 235
STUDY 12 — Resurrection & Commission _______ 241
CLOSING CELEBRATION SESSION: From Eyewitness to Witness ______________________ 247

Seeing the Whole Story —Six Sermons that Really Matter

When you hold *Eyewitness: The Life of Christ Told in One Story* in your hands, you're reading much more than a devotional narrative. This is all the information from the Gospels and other Bible verses compiled into a chronological revealing of God's plan for us through the Jesus life from the beginning to his ultimate sacrifice for our sins.

You are stepping into a carefully assembled testimony. The purpose of *Eyewitness* is clear: to arrange the Gospel accounts into one chronological, cohesive story so we can see the life of Jesus in its fullness rather than in fragments.

- The four Gospels give us truth.
- *Eyewitness* gives us sequence.
- The six sermons give us focus.

If *Eyewitness* answers the question, *What happened?* these six messages answer the question, *What does Jesus' coming mean?*

From Narrative to Transformation

The Gospels were written by eyewitnesses and early investigators. They saw. They heard. They touched. They testified. *Eyewitness* gathers those testimonies and arranges them into one seamless account so we can follow Jesus step-by-step—from eternity past to ascension glory.

But information alone doesn't transform.

You can know the chronology of Christ's life and still miss the heart of it. You can follow the timeline and still fail to follow the Savior.

That is why these six sermons exist.

They are not replacements for the *Eyewitness* book. They are companions to it.

They are designed to:

- Illuminate the major movements of Jesus' life.
- Highlight the central theological themes.
- Call the listener from observation to participation.
- Move from history to surrender.

If *Eyewitness* helps people see the whole forest, these sermons invite them to walk among the trees.

Six Movements of Redemption

The life of Christ isn't random. It unfolds with divine precision. These six sermons trace the grand arc of redemption revealed in *Eyewitness*.

1. The Light That Darkness Could Not Overcome

The story begins before Bethlehem. Before Nazareth. Before Rome. It begins in eternity.

Jesus isn't introduced as a moral teacher but as the eternal Word, the Creator, the Light who stepped into darkness. This message establishes identity. If we misunderstand who Jesus is, we will misunderstand everything else about him.

This sermon anchors the entire journey in one foundational truth:

Jesus is not merely part of the story—he is the source of it.

2. Heaven Interrupts the Ordinary

From Zechariah in the Temple to Mary in Nazareth, from shepherds in fields to Simeon and Anna in the Temple courts, heaven breaks into common lives.

This message explores divine interruption.

Redemption did not begin in palaces but in obedience. It shows how God accomplishes extraordinary purposes through ordinary faithfulness.

When heaven steps into the ordinary, the only question that matters is this:

Will we cling to our plans or surrender to the extraordinary purpose God is unfolding?

3. The Voice in the Wilderness

Before revelation comes preparation.

John the Baptizer stands in the wilderness crying, "Prepare the way." This sermon examines repentance, readiness, and the necessity of spiritual preparation before fully encountering Christ.

It reminds us that you can't receive the King while clinging to rebellion.

If we truly long to see the King in his fullness, we must first clear the path in our own hearts. Why?

Because Christ does not force his way into lives that refuse to make room for him.

4. The Kingdom Revealed

As Jesus begins his ministry—teaching, healing, confronting religious corruption, forgiving sinners—the Kingdom of God is unveiled.

This message explores:

- The authority of Christ.
- The nature of the Kingdom.
- The difference between religion and relationship.

- Grace and truth working together.

Here, listeners are confronted, not just with miracles, but with the claims of Christ.

5. The Cross: Where Darkness Thought It Won

The narrative moves toward Jerusalem. Toward betrayal. Toward trial. Toward crucifixion.

This sermon centers on the heart of redemption. The Lamb of God takes away the sin of the world. What seemed like defeat was victory. What looked like darkness was divine purpose.

The cross is not an unfortunate ending. It is the fulfillment of everything that preceded it.

6. The Risen Lord and the Living Hope

The tomb is opened. Witnesses see. Fear turns to joy. Doubt turns to worship.

This final message declares that resurrection changes everything:

- Death doesn't win.
- Sin doesn't have the last word.
- Hope isn't theoretical. It's embodied in a living Savior.

The story that began with Light ends with Commission.

The One who came now sends.

From Observation to Participation

One of the unique strengths of *Eyewitness* is its clarity. It arranges events so readers can visualize the life of Christ as one unfolding reality.

But these sermons press further.

They ask:

- Where are you in this story?
- Are you observing the Light—or walking in it?

- Are you hearing the voice—or preparing your heart?
- Are you admiring the cross—or trusting it?
- Are you celebrating the resurrection—or living under its authority?

The purpose isn't merely to understand Jesus chronologically.

The purpose is to encounter him personally.

A Journey, Not Just a Study

The subtitle of the sermon series says it well: *A Journey Through the Life of Christ.*

A journey implies movement.

You don't journey to stay where you started.

As these six messages unfold, they follow the chronology of *Eyewitness* while drawing out the central redemptive themes that run through every chapter:

- Light breaking darkness.
- Heaven invading earth.
- Repentance preceding revelation.
- Authority confronting religion.
- Sacrifice securing redemption.
- Resurrection launching mission.

Each sermon stands on its own, but together they form one unified declaration: Jesus Christ is the eternal Son of God who entered history, fulfilled prophecy, and bore our sin. He conquered death and now calls us to follow him.

Why This Matters Now

Consider the possibilities:

- It's possible to admire Jesus historically and ignore him personally.

- It's possible to study the Gospels academically and miss their transforming power.
- It's possible to read the story and never surrender to the Savior.

The six sermons are meant to prevent that.

- They are not simply explanatory.
  They are invitational.
- They don't merely recount what happened.
  They ask what will happen in you.

The Invitation Ahead

As you move from the pages of *Eyewitness* into these six messages, approach them prayerfully.

Ask:

- What does this reveal about who Jesus truly is?
- What does this expose in my own heart?
- What obedience is being called for?
- What darkness must give way to Light?

The eyewitnesses saw him.
The Scriptures testify about him.
This book arranges his story.
These sermons proclaim his meaning.
Now, the question becomes personal: Will you walk with him?

- The journey begins with Light.
- It moves through surrender.
- It passes by a cross.
- It ends in resurrection hope.

And it continues in every life that says yes.

SERMON 1:
Light That Darkness Couldn't Overcome

Theme: Jesus is the eternal Light who stepped into our darkness to reveal God and make us children of God.

Key Texts: John 1:1–18; Isaiah 9:2; Genesis 1:1–3

Eyewitness Chapters

"Eyewitnesses begin their amazing testimony" to "The ancestry of Jesus is recorded."

Introduction: When the Light Breaks In

Imagine being lowered into a cavern so deep that no sunlight has ever touched its walls. The air is cold. The silence is thick. You stretch your hands in front of your face and can't see them. You try to walk, but every step feels uncertain. You don't know what you might stumble over. You don't know what might be hiding in the darkness.

Then someone strikes a single match.

It's astonishing how small a flame can be—and how powerless darkness is against it.

- Darkness doesn't fight back.
- Darkness doesn't push forward.
- Darkness doesn't resist.
- Darkness retreats.

John begins his Gospel, not with shepherds or wise men, not with Bethlehem or Nazareth—but with light breaking into darkness.

The *Eyewitness* account opens this way:

"The Word already existed. He was with God, and he was God, in the beginning. Everything was created by him. Nothing existed that he did not make. Life itself came from him, and this life gave light to everyone. When God said, 'Let there be light,' the light shone in the darkness, and the darkness could not overcome it."

- This isn't merely poetry.
- This is reality beyond what we can see or fully understand.
- This is eternity breaking into time.

Today we are going to stand at the beginning—not of a book, but of reality itself—and see what it means that Jesus is the Light that darkness could not overcome.

Before There Was a Beginning

"In the beginning…"

Those three words take us back before Bethlehem. Before Abraham. Before Moses. Before David. Before Rome. Before creation.

Genesis says, "In the beginning, God created the heavens and the earth."

John says, "The Word already existed."

- Before there was a star in the sky, the Word already existed.
- Before there was a molecule in motion, the Word already existed.
- Before there was sin to forgive, the Word already existed.

John doesn't present Jesus as a religious teacher who appeared at a moment in history. He presents him as the eternal Creator who stepped into our timeline.

"The Word was with God, and he was God."

- Not created by God.
- Not second to God.
- Not a lesser being.

He was with God—and he was God. If that is true—and it is—then everything changes.

- If Jesus is merely a teacher, you can debate him.
- If Jesus is merely a prophet, you can compare him.
- If Jesus is merely a moral example, you can admire him.

But if Jesus is God in the flesh—you must bow.

The text says, "Everything was created by him. Nothing existed that he did not make."

- The mountains? He made them.
- The oceans? He spoke to them.
- The galaxies beyond our telescopes? He flung them into space.

And here is the staggering truth: The One who created everything entered his own creation.

- That means the manger was holding the Maker of Stars.
- That means the carpenter in Nazareth designed the forests of Lebanon.
- That means the hands that would be nailed to a cross shaped Adam from dust.

This isn't sentimental religion. This is cosmic reality. And it means something deeply personal:

- Your life isn't random.
- Your existence isn't accidental.
- Your story isn't a mistake.

The One who made everything made you.

Genesis tells us that in the beginning, "the earth was a formless void covered by darkness."

Darkness isn't just the absence of light. It's chaos, confusion, and emptiness.

Then God said, "Let there be light."

And light came.

Now, John picks up that same imagery and applies it to Jesus:

"Life itself came from him, and this life gave light to everyone."

Light in Scripture symbolizes revelation. Truth. Purity. Hope.

Darkness symbolizes ignorance. Sin. Fear. Separation.

And John says, "The light shone in the darkness, and the darkness could not overcome it."

Notice what it doesn't say.

- It doesn't say darkness challenged the light.
- It doesn't say darkness resisted the light.
- It doesn't say darkness pushed back against the light.

It says darkness could not overcome it.

Why?

Because darkness isn't an active force. It's simply the absence of light.

When light appears, darkness has no defense.

This isn't just cosmology. It's salvation.

The world was not just morally confused. It was spiritually dark.

Isaiah prophesied: "People who walk in darkness will see a bright light. Upon those who live under dark shadows of death, the light will shine."

Think of the darkness into which Jesus was born:

- Political oppression under Rome.

- Religious corruption in the Temple.
- Moral decay in society.
- Personal brokenness in homes.

And yet John declares: "The light shone."

- Light doesn't wait for darkness to improve.
- Light doesn't wait for darkness to cooperate.
- Light simply shines.

When Jesus entered the world, he did not enter as a philosopher offering ideas.

He entered as Light revealing truth.

He revealed:

- Who God is.
- Who we are.
- What sin does.
- What grace offers.

The difference between darkness and light is the difference between night and day.

- Darkness hides. Light exposes.
- Darkness confuses. Light clarifies.
- Darkness enslaves. Light frees.

The question isn't whether light has come.

The question is whether we will step into it.

The Tragedy of Not Recognizing Jesus

One of the most heartbreaking lines in the opening of John is this: "Although the Word made the world, people in the world did not recognize him when he came."

The Creator walked among his creation—and was unrecognized.

- He healed their sick.
- He fed their hungry.

- He raised their dead.
- He fulfilled their prophecies.

And still—they didn't recognize him.

Why?

Because darkness prefers familiarity to revelation.

- Light exposes pride.
- Light exposes hypocrisy.
- Light exposes sin.

And people love their darkness.

Later in the Gospel, Jesus would say: "Light has come into the world, but people love the darkness, not the light, because their deeds are evil."

This isn't an ancient problem. It's a current one.

- We can be religious and still not recognize him.
- We can attend services and still not recognize him.
- We can quote verses and still not recognize him.

Recognizing Jesus isn't intellectual acknowledgment. It's surrender.

When light shines into your heart, it reveals what you would rather hide.

And that is uncomfortable.

But hear this clearly: Light exposes, not to condemn, but to heal.

When a surgeon turns on a bright light in an operating room, it isn't to shame the patient. It's to save them.

When Jesus shines light into your life, he isn't humiliating you. He is rescuing you.

The Word Became Flesh

John then says something utterly breathtaking: "The Word became human and lived among his own people."

- The eternal stepped into time.

- The infinite entered finiteness.
- The invisible became visible.

Jesus did not send a message. He came *himself*.

- He did not shout instructions from Heaven. He walked our streets.
- He did not observe suffering from a distance. He entered into it.

The Word became flesh.
That means:

- He felt hunger.
- He felt fatigue.
- He felt rejection.
- He felt betrayal.
- He felt pain.

He did not pretend to be human. He was fully human.
And yet… fully God.
This is the miracle of incarnation.

And the text says: "No one has ever seen God. However, his Son, Jesus, who came from him, has revealed him to us."

If you want to know what God is like—look at Jesus.

- When Jesus touches a leper—that is what God is like.
- When Jesus forgives a sinner—that is what God is like.
- When Jesus weeps at a tomb—that is what God is like.
- When Jesus stretches out his arms on a cross—that is what God is like.

Where is God in relation to where we are?

- God isn't distant.
- God isn't indifferent.
- God isn't detached.
- God came to be *with* us.

John contrasts two realities: "Moses gave us the Law, but Jesus Christ gave us grace and truth."

What did the Law accomplish?

- The Law revealed what righteousness looks like—but couldn't empower us to live it.
- The Law exposed sin—but couldn't remove it.

What does Grace do for us?

- Grace doesn't ignore truth.
  Grace fulfills truth.
- Truth without grace crushes.
  Grace without truth deceives.

Jesus brought both.

He told the woman caught in adultery, "Go and sin no more." That is truth.

He also said, "Neither do I condemn you." That is grace.

- He didn't lower the standard.
- He lifted the sinner.

And this is crucial:

If you try to approach God only through Law, you will live in fear.

If you approach God through Grace, you will live in transformation.

- Grace isn't permission to sin.
- Grace is power to change.

The Right to Become Children

Perhaps the most astonishing promise in the opening chapter of John is this: "But he gave those who believed and accepted him the right to become God's children."

- Not servants.
- Not spectators.
- Children.

Belief isn't mere agreement. Belief is trust.

Acceptance isn't passive awareness. It's reception.

When you receive Christ, you are not signing up for religion. You are entering relationship.

You are adopted.

- Adoption is intentional.
- Adoption is chosen.
- Adoption is permanent.

John says we are born again "not physically out of human desire but spiritually by the will of God."

This isn't self-improvement. This is new birth.

- You can't educate yourself into spiritual life.
- You can't discipline yourself into spiritual life.
- You can't inherit yourself into spiritual life.

You must be born again.

And that birth comes through the Light.

The Eyewitness Testimony

The introduction closes by emphasizing testimony: "The eyewitnesses have seen the majestic splendor of Jesus Christ … with their own eyes, touched him with their own hands, and heard him with their own ears … People have carefully investigated all these accounts, so you may be certain that this record is accurate."

- This isn't myth.
- This isn't legend.
- This is testimony.

Christianity doesn't ask you to suspend reason. It invites you to examine the evidence.

- They saw him.
- They touched him.
- They heard him.

And they were willing to die for what they saw.

Light doesn't need defense.

It simply needs to be seen.

Application: Where Is the Darkness?

Let me ask you plainly: Where is the darkness in your life?

- Is it hidden sin?
- Is it bitterness?
- Is it fear?
- Is it unbelief?
- Is it shame from the past?

The Light has come.

Darkness can't overcome it.

But here is the sobering truth: Darkness can be preferred.

Some people would rather live in familiar darkness than risk stepping into exposing light.

But the Light did not come to destroy you. It came to rescue you.

It came to reveal truth so you could be free.

Call to Response

The Light is shining.

Will you:

- Recognize him?
- Receive him?
- Walk in him?

You don't fight darkness by swinging at it.

You fight darkness by turning on the light.

Today, you can step into that light.

You can say: "Jesus, you are the eternal Word. You are the Light. I believe. I receive. Make me your child."

And the darkness can't hold you.

Closing Emphasis

The story of Jesus is more than a moment in history. It's Light shining from eternity past and still shining today.

Before creation—he was.

At creation—he spoke.

In history—he came.

At the cross—he redeemed.

From the tomb—he rose.

In your life—he shines.

"The light shone in the darkness, and the darkness could not overcome it."

Darkness tried at Calvary.

Darkness sealed a tomb.

Darkness thought it had won.

But Sunday morning proved the truth.

The Light can't be extinguished.

And if the Light lives in you—the darkness in this world can't overcome you either.

Step into the Light. And live.

SERMON 2:
Heaven Interrupts the Ordinary

Theme: God enters ordinary lives to accomplish extraordinary redemption.

Key Texts: Luke 1–2; Matthew 1

Eyewitness Chapters

"An angel meets Zechariah in the Temple" to "The Holy Spirit leads Jesus to an encounter with Satan."

Introduction: When Heaven Breaks into a Tuesday

Most of life feels ordinary.

- We wake up.
- We go to work.
- We run errands.
- We answer emails.
- We pay bills.
- We fix dinner.
- We go to bed.

History rarely announces itself in advance.

No one wakes up and says, "Today will be the day that changes the world."

Yet when you open the Gospel narrative, you discover something astonishing:

The greatest turning point in human history did not begin in a palace.

- It did not begin in a temple.
- It did not begin in Rome.
- It began in obscurity.
- It began with a priest burning incense.
- It began with a young woman in Nazareth.
- It began with a carpenter trying to do the right thing.
- It began with shepherds working a night shift.

Heaven did not wait for extraordinary settings. Heaven interrupted the ordinary.

The *Eyewitness* account records the angel Gabriel's words to Mary: "Do not be frightened, Mary. God is pleased with you. … Nothing is impossible with God."

That isn't merely a comforting phrase.

It's a declaration of divine intrusion.

Today we are going to see how heaven breaks into ordinary lives—and what it requires when it does.

God Chooses the Overlooked

The story doesn't begin with Mary. It begins with Zechariah.

The text tells us that Zechariah was "a man of the priestly order … upright in God's sight."

He was doing what priests do. Burning incense. Offering prayers. Serving faithfully.

And suddenly: "An angel appeared, and Zechariah was paralyzed with fear."

The first lesson we learn is this: Heaven often interrupts faithfulness, not fame.

- Zechariah was not leading a revival.
- He was not performing miracles.
- He was serving quietly.

Many believers think breakthroughs come when they become visible.

But heaven broke into the Temple, not because Zechariah was famous, but because he was faithful.

Let me say something to you gently: God doesn't overlook quiet obedience.

- You may think your life is unnoticed.
- You may think your prayers are unheard.
- You may think your faithfulness is invisible.

But heaven sees what the world ignores.

The angel says: "God has heard your prayer."

Those words had been decades in the making.

Elizabeth was barren and beyond the normal age for having children.

Zechariah was too old to have any reasonable hope for a son.

And yet—God had heard.

Sometimes, God's silence isn't absence. It's preparation.

Zechariah says: "How can this be? This is impossible."

That sounds familiar, doesn't it?

Heaven declares possibility.

We answer with probability.

Heaven says, "I will."

We say, "But…"

The angel replies: "Because you have not believed me, you will be unable to speak."

There are moments when doubt silences us.

But even in Zechariah's hesitation, God doesn't withdraw his promise.

He disciplines—but he fulfills.

Heaven interrupts ordinary life—but heaven also demands faith.

Now, the scene shifts.

- Not to Jerusalem.
- Not to royalty.
- Not to power.

To Nazareth.

Nazareth was not impressive. It was small. Unremarkable. Dismissed.

Into that setting steps Gabriel again. "Greetings, favored woman. God is with you."

Mary is shaken.

The text says she trembled.

This isn't a sentimental nativity scene.

This is a young virgin being told her entire life is about to change.

"You will become pregnant and give birth to a son. You must name him Jesus."

And then the angel says something extraordinary: "The Holy Spirit will come upon you … Nothing is impossible with God."

What is God's promise to Mary?

- She isn't promised comfort.
- She isn't promised convenience.
- She isn't promised reputation.
- She is promised purpose.

And then comes one of the most powerful responses in Scripture: "I am God's servant … Let all you have said happen to me according to his will."

Notice the contrast:

- Zechariah: "How can this be?" He asked for explanation.

- Mary: "Let it be." She offered surrender.

This is the difference between control and calling.
When heaven interrupts, it doesn't negotiate details.
It invites trust.

Mary did not know:

- How Joseph would respond.
- How her community would react.
- What the future would cost.

But she knew this: If God is speaking, obedience is safer than resistance.

If God interrupted your plans this week, how would you respond?

- Would you say, "Explain it first"?
- Would you say, "Prove it"?
- Or would you say, "Let it be"?

Most of us want clarity before obedience.
But heaven often gives obedience before clarity.
Mary's surrender did not eliminate difficulty.
It positioned her for divine partnership.

Joseph — The Quiet Obedience of a Righteous Man

Now, the spotlight shifts again—to Joseph.
What do we know about him?

- He isn't dramatic.
- He isn't vocal.
- He is steady.

The text says: "When Joseph discovered that his fiancée was pregnant, he did not want to subject her to public disgrace."

- He chooses mercy over exposure.

- He chooses quiet righteousness over public anger.

Then heaven interrupts him in a dream: "Joseph, son of David, do not be afraid to get married … The child has been conceived … by the Holy Spirit."

Joseph wakes up.

And the text says: "He did as the angel had commanded."

- No speech recorded.
- No song recorded.
- No protest recorded.
- Just obedience.

Some of the most powerful faith is silent faith.

Joseph embraces:

- Social misunderstanding
- Personal risk
- Financial burden
- Emotional uncertainty

Why?

Because heaven interrupted his ordinary plans.

He thought he was building a simple life.

God was building a redemptive history.

Joseph never preaches a sermon.

He never performs a miracle.

He never writes a book.

But he protects the Messiah.

Don't underestimate hidden obedience.

Some of you are protecting purposes you can't yet see.

Stay faithful.

Glory in the Fields

Now, the setting moves to shepherds.

Shepherds were not prestigious.

- They smelled like sheep.
- They worked night shifts.
- They were overlooked.

And suddenly: "An angel of God appeared in brilliant light."

The angel says: "Do not be afraid. My good news will bring great joy to everyone."

And then heaven can't contain itself: "Glory to God in the highest, and on Earth peace, good will toward men."

- Heaven doesn't announce to Caesar.
- Heaven doesn't announce to Herod.
- Heaven announces to shepherds.

Why?

Because the Gospel isn't reserved for elites.

Even the priests and teachers of the Law didn't get the birth announcement.

Shepherds who tended sheep destined for Temple sacrifices received word about the Lamb of God, destined for sacrifice for our sins.

The shepherds respond immediately:

- They go.
- They see.
- They worship.
- They tell.

Heaven interrupts.

Faith responds.

Witness follows.

Simeon — Waiting in the Temple

When Mary and Joseph bring Jesus to the Temple, they meet Simeon.

The text says he was righteous and waiting.

The Spirit had promised that he would see the Messiah before he died.

When he holds the infant, he says: "With my own eyes, I have seen your salvation prepared for all people."

Notice something:

- He does not say, "I have seen a baby."
- He says, "I have seen salvation."

Salvation isn't an event.
Salvation is a Person.
Heaven interrupts waiting hearts.
Some of you have been waiting a long time.
Do not mistake delay for denial.
Simeon waited faithfully—and heaven fulfilled precisely.

Anna — The Persistence of Devotion

Anna is eighty-four.

- She fasts.
- She prays.
- She stays in the Temple.

And when she sees the infant Jesus, she praises God and declares redemption.

Heaven honors long obedience.
Do not underestimate decades of devotion.
You may not see the full story until the final chapter.
But heaven sees.

The Meaning of the Interruption

Why did heaven interrupt?

- Because humanity couldn't rescue itself.
- Because the Law couldn't redeem.
- Because ritual couldn't save.
- Because power couldn't transform.

Heaven entered time.

God stepped into flesh.

This isn't God improving our system.

This is God replacing it.

Heaven interrupts ordinary life because ordinary life can't redeem itself.

Application: What Is God Interrupting in you?

What if the frustration you are experiencing isn't punishment—but redirection?

What if the closed door isn't rejection—but protection?

What if the unexpected season isn't delay—but preparation?

Heaven interrupts the ordinary to accomplish the eternal.

Mary's yes brought salvation into history.

Joseph's obedience protected the Messiah.

The shepherds' witness spread the news.

Simeon's waiting testified to fulfillment.

Anna's devotion confirmed redemption.

What is your role?

Call to Response

The miracle of Christmas was not a one-time interruption in history. Heaven still breaks into ordinary lives.

Heaven still interrupts.

- Not with angels in fields—
  But with conviction in hearts.
- Not with audible voices—
  But with inward prompting.

The question isn't whether God is speaking.

The question is whether you will answer like Mary: "I am your servant."

You may not understand the future.

But you can trust the One who holds it.

Closing Emphasis

The greatest moments in God's story often begin on the most ordinary days.

On an ordinary day—

- A priest burned incense.
- A young woman trembled.
- A carpenter slept.
- Shepherds watched sheep.
- An elderly man waited.
- And heaven broke in.
- History changed.
- Redemption began.

The same God who interrupted Nazareth and Bethlehem can interrupt your ordinary life—and make it part of something eternal.

Nothing is impossible with God.

Say yes.

Let heaven interrupt.

SERMON 3:
The Voice in the Wilderness

Theme: Preparation precedes revelation.

Key Texts: Isaiah 40:3–5; Malachi 3:1; Matthew 3; John 1

Eyewitness Chapters

"John the Baptizer recognizes Jesus as the Lamb of God."

Introduction: The Sound Before the Arrival

Every important moment in life is preceded by preparation.

- Before a king arrives, roads are repaired.
- Before a surgeon operates, the instruments are sterilized.
- Before a harvest is gathered, the soil is prepared.
- Before revelation comes—preparation must occur.

The Gospel doesn't introduce Jesus publicly until it first introduces a voice. Not a king. Not a miracle worker. A voice.

The *Eyewitness* account says: "The word of God came to John, son of Zechariah, in the wilderness."

Notice where the word came.

- Not to Jerusalem.
- Not to the Temple hierarchy.
- Not to the powerful.

It came in the wilderness.

And it came to a man who wore camel's hair and ate locusts and wild honey.

That alone should tell us something profound: God often prepares great movements in obscure places.

Today, we are going to stand in the wilderness with John the Baptizer and listen carefully. Because his message was not merely historical. It's deeply personal.

If we want to encounter Christ in fullness, we must understand the necessity of preparation.

The Wilderness — Preparation Ground, Not a Detour

The text says: "The word of God came to John … in the wilderness."

The wilderness in Scripture is never accidental.

- Israel wandered there.
- Moses was shaped there.
- Elijah was strengthened there.
- Jesus himself would be led there.

The wilderness is where distractions are stripped away.

- It's where identity is clarified.
- It's where dependency is formed.

John did not launch his ministry in comfort. He was forged in solitude.

Let us consider something carefully: John had priestly heritage.

- He could have served in the Temple like his father.
- He could have pursued influence within religious systems.

Instead, he withdrew.

Why?

Because before you can speak clearly to a generation, you must hear clearly from God.

Noise weakens discernment.

Crowds can distort calling.

The wilderness protects purity.

The wilderness is preparation, not punishment.

Some of you are in a wilderness season right now.

- It feels quiet.
- It feels unseen.
- It feels slow.

But heaven may be shaping you.

God doesn't waste our wilderness experiences.

The Message — "Repent"

When John begins preaching, his message is direct: "Repent, for the Kingdom of Heaven is near."

That word *repent* is often misunderstood.

It doesn't merely mean "feel sorry."

It means…

- To change direction.
- To turn around.
- To reorient your life toward God.

John isn't offering inspiration.

He isn't offering self-improvement.

He *is* demanding transformation.

The prophecy he fulfills says: "Clear a path in the wilderness … Fill the valleys and flatten the mountains. Straighten the curves and smooth the rough places."

This imagery is powerful.

When a king traveled, roads were prepared ahead of him. Obstacles were removed. Paths were made straight.

John is saying the King is coming, so we need to prepare the roads of our hearts.

What does that mean?

- Valleys filled — places of despair lifted.
- Mountains lowered — pride humbled.
- Crooked paths straightened — deception corrected.
- Rough places smoothed — bitterness softened.

Repentance isn't cosmetic adjustment.

It's road construction.

The Kingdom can't fully enter a heart cluttered with rebellion.

If Christ feels distant, sometimes the issue is our preparation, not his presence.

What in your heart is blocking the road?

- Is it pride?
- Is it secret sin?
- Is it unforgiveness?
- Is it complacency?
- Is it self-reliance?

Preparation precedes revelation.

John did not introduce Jesus until he had called the people to repentance.

- We want revival without repentance.
- We want breakthrough without surrender.
- We want blessing without alignment.

But heaven doesn't bypass preparation.

Authentic Repentance Bears Fruit

The crowds respond to John.

They confess their sins. They are baptized.

But John discerns something troubling: "You bunch of snakes. Who warned you to flee God's judgment? The way you live proves whether you have left your sins and turned to God."

That isn't seeker-sensitive language.

But it *is* Spirit-sensitive language.

John understands something vital: External participation doesn't equal internal transformation.

He says: "Do not say … 'We are Abraham's descendants.' That doesn't mean anything."

- Heritage can't substitute for repentance.
- Tradition can't replace obedience.
- Association can't equal transformation.

True repentance produces fruit.

The people ask: "What should we do?"

And John answers practically:

- If you have two garments, give one away.
- Share your food.
- Do not exploit others.
- Be content.

Repentance touches behavior.

If nothing changes, nothing has been changed.

Preparation isn't emotional. It's structural.

If Christ is near—there should be evidence.

- Has your speech softened?
- Has your generosity increased?
- Has your honesty strengthened?
- Has your compassion grown?

The Kingdom isn't theoretical.

It reshapes conduct.

As John's ministry grows, people begin asking: "Are you the Messiah?"

Imagine the temptation.

- Crowds are gathering.
- Influence is increasing.
- Authority is recognized.

But John says: "No, I am not the Messiah."

He goes further: "I am not worthy to stoop down and untie the straps of his sandals."

Humility protects preparation.

John understands his role.

- He isn't the Light.
- He is a *witness* to the Light.
- He isn't the Lamb.
- He *announces* the Lamb.

John later declares: "Look! The Lamb of God, who takes away the sin of the world."

That is the climax of preparation.

Preparation is never about the messenger.

It's about the arrival of Christ.

If your life is truly prepared, it will point away from you and toward him.

- When God begins using you, humility must deepen.
- When influence increases, surrender must increase.
- Preparation doesn't end when revelation comes.

It must continue.

The Baptism of Jesus — Identity Before Ministry

When Jesus comes to be baptized, John hesitates: "I should be baptized by you."

But Jesus responds: "This is what should be done. We must do all that God requires of us."

Then something extraordinary happens: "The Spirit of God descended like a dove … A voice spoke from above: 'You are my son, whom I love. I am well pleased with you.'"

Notice something deeply important.

This affirmation happens before Jesus performs a single miracle.

- Before public acclaim.
- Before sermons.
- Before crowds.

Identity precedes activity.

Preparation precedes demonstration.

The Father affirms the Son in quiet obedience.

If we don't secure identity in the Father's love, we will seek validation in performance.

Preparation anchors identity.

The Wilderness Temptations

Immediately after baptism, Jesus is led into the wilderness.

Preparation is tested.

The tempter says: "Since you are the Son of God…"

Notice the strategy.

The Father just said, "You are my Son."

The enemy says, "Since you are…"

Temptation always attacks identity.

And Jesus responds with Scripture.

Preparation shows in response.

If the heart has been shaped in wilderness, temptation doesn't derail calling.

Preparation strengthens resistance.

The Central Announcement — The Lamb

John sees Jesus and says: "Look! The Lamb of God, who takes away the sin of the world."

This revelation is staggering. Who is Jesus?

- Not a reformer.
- Not a revolutionary.
- Not a philosopher.
- The Lamb.

The Lamb represents sacrifice.

Preparation was not simply moral. It was sacrificial.

The King would come, not to dominate, but to redeem.

Repentance prepares us to receive a Saviour, not merely a teacher.

Application: Are you Ready for Revelation?

The tragedy of many believers isn't ignorance. It's unpreparedness.

- We ask for fresh revelation.
  But have we cleared the road?
- We ask for deeper encounters.
  But have we humbled pride?
- We ask for revival.
  But have we repented?

Preparation precedes revelation.

Call to Response

Today, the voice still cries in the wilderness.

- Prepare.

- Repent.
- Realign.

Christ is near.

- Let valleys be lifted.
- Let mountains fall.
- Let crooked paths straighten.
- Let rough places soften.

Prepare your heart.

Closing Emphasis

Every great movement of God begins with preparation.
Before the miracles—there was repentance.
Before the crowds—there was wilderness.
Before the revelation—there was preparation.
John's voice still echoes: "Prepare the way."
The King has come.
Clear the road.
And let him enter fully.

SERMON 4:
Come and See

Theme: Discipleship begins with invitation and grows through surrender, transformation, and witness.

Key Texts: John 1:35–51; John 2; John 4

Eyewitness Chapters

"Disciples of John the Baptizer meet Jesus for the first time" to "A Samaritan woman comes for water and finds life."

Introduction: The Power of an Invitation

Some of the most life-changing moments in history begin with two simple words: "Come and see."

- Not an argument.
- Not a debate.
- Not a theological lecture.
- An invitation.
- A door opened.
- A hand extended.
- A step taken.

When we first encounter Jesus in his public ministry, that is exactly how it begins—not with spectacle, not with thunder—but with invitation.

The *Eyewitness* account records two men following Jesus and asking where he was staying.

What did Jesus say? "Come and see."

Those words still echo across centuries.

Today, we will consider that invitation: "Come and see."

We are going to trace how discipleship unfolds.

- From curiosity to calling.
- From encounter to transformation.
- From private faith to public witness.

Christianity doesn't begin with mastery of doctrine. It begins with encounter.

It begins with "Come and see."

The Invitation — Curiosity Becomes Pursuit

The setting is the Jordan River.

John the Baptizer has just declared: "Look! The Lamb of God."

Two of his disciples hear him: Andrew and John.

They do something simple but profound.

They follow Jesus.

They are not yet apostles.

They are not yet leaders.

They are seekers.

And Jesus turns and asks: "What do you want?"

That is a significant question.

- He doesn't ask, "Do you understand?"
- He doesn't ask, "Are you qualified?"
- He asks, "What do you want?"

Why?

Because desire precedes discipleship.

Many people admire Jesus.

Fewer pursue him.

Andrew and John don't offer a theological statement. They ask: "Where are you staying?"

- They want proximity.
- They want presence.
- They want to know him—not just know about him.

And Jesus says: "Come and see."

- He doesn't overwhelm them.
- He doesn't outline a five-year plan.
- He doesn't give them a syllabus.
- He invites them into relationship.

Discipleship begins with closeness, not complexity.

What do you want from Jesus?

- Do you want relief?
- Do you want answers?
- Do you want blessings?
- Do you want reputation?
- Or do you want *him*?

Desire determines direction.

- If you want comfort, you will follow until discomfort comes.
- If you want clarity, you will follow until mystery appears.
- But if you want him—you will follow through confusion, hardship, and growth.

Andrew wanted proximity.

The text tells us: "It was about ten o'clock in the morning … and they spent the day with him."

A day that changed history.

Do not underestimate what can happen in a single day with Jesus.

Something remarkable happens next.

Andrew doesn't keep the encounter to himself.

The *Eyewitness* record says: "Before John reached his brother James, Andrew reached his own brother Simon and said, 'We have found the Messiah.'"

Notice the order.

- Encounter.
- Conviction.
- Declaration.

Notice what he says:

- He doesn't say, "We have found a teacher."
- He doesn't say, "We have found a moral example."
- He does say, "We have found the Messiah."

He brings Simon to Jesus.

That is evangelism in its simplest form.

- Not argument.
- Not coercion.
- An invitation.

And then Jesus does something profound.

He looks at Simon and says: "You are Simon … you will be called Cephas … Rock."

Jesus renames him.

- Before Simon preaches.
- Before he fails.
- Before he denies.
- Before he leads.

Jesus declares his future identity, in sharp contrast to who he was.

That is what happens when you come and see.

Jesus doesn't merely accept who you are.

He reveals who you will become.

Some of you are living under old names.

- Failure.
- Addict.
- Broken.
- Unworthy.
- Forgotten.

When you encounter Jesus, he renames your destiny.

You are not defined by your past.

You are defined by his calling.

Discipleship isn't self-improvement.

It's identity transformation.

The Skeptic — Nathanael Under the Fig Tree

The next day, Jesus calls Philip.

Philip immediately finds Nathanael and says: "We've found the one Moses wrote about … Jesus … from Nazareth."

Nathanael responds honestly: "Nazareth? Can anything good come from there?"

Skepticism isn't new.

But notice Philip's answer: "Come see for yourself."

- He doesn't argue geography.
- He doesn't defend Nazareth.
- He invites experience.

When Nathanael approaches, Jesus says: "Behold, a true Israelite in whom is no deceit."

Nathanael is startled. "How can you know me?"

Jesus replies: "I saw you while you were still under the fig tree."

We are not told what happened under that tree.

Perhaps Nathanael was praying.

Perhaps wrestling with Scripture.

Most likely, he was meditating on a passage about the Messiah.

What did Jesus know?

- What Nathanael was thinking.
- Where Nathanael was at that time.

And Nathanael responds: "You really are the Son of God."

Here is the pattern again:

- Invitation.
- Encounter.
- Recognition.

There are moments in your life that no one else witnessed.

- Private prayers.
- Silent tears.
- Unspoken doubts.

Jesus sees.

And when he reveals that he sees, faith ignites.

He doesn't merely know facts about you.

He knows you.

That is why discipleship can't remain intellectual.

It becomes personal.

Cana — From Invitation to Revelation

Three days later, Jesus attends a wedding.

- Not a revival meeting.
- Not a religious summit.

- A wedding.

And the wine runs out.
Mary says: "They have no more wine."
Jesus replies: "My time has not yet come."
Until the time came, Jesus didn't know it was time.
He instructs the servants: "Fill the jars with water."
And then: "The water … had been turned into wine."

The *Eyewitness* account concludes: "This miracle … was the first sign of Jesus' majesty, and his disciples believed in him."

Notice something vital:

- Belief deepens after revelation.
- The disciples already followed him.
- But now their faith strengthens.

Discipleship grows through progressive revelation.

- You come.
- You see.
- You believe.
- You grow.

Obedience precedes understanding.
Mary told the servants: "Do whatever he tells you."
That is discipleship in a single sentence.
Fill jars with water—even if it seems ordinary.
Transformation often begins with simple obedience.

The Samaritan Woman — Invitation Beyond Boundaries

Now, we move to John, Chapter 4.
Jesus goes through Samaria.
That was unusual.
Jews avoided Samaritans.
Yet Jesus stops at a well.

He asks a woman: "Would you give me a drink?"

She is surprised.

Conversation unfolds.

He offers: "Living water … a fresh artesian spring, bubbling with everlasting life."

He reveals her history.

Five husbands.

Current dysfunctional relationship.

He doesn't shame her.

He exposes truth to offer life.

Then he declares: "I am the Messiah."

She leaves her water jar.

Runs to spread the news: "Come see a man who told me everything I ever did."

Again—invitation.

And the people say: "We have seen and heard for ourselves … He really is the Savior of the world."

Discipleship overflows.

When you encounter living water, you can't keep silent.

The text notes something subtle but powerful.

- She left her water jar.
- The thing she came *for* became secondary.

When you encounter Christ, old priorities lose their grip.

What water jar are you clinging to?

- Career?
- Reputation?
- Comfort?
- Approval?

Leave it.

Run tell others.

The Harvest Vision

After the woman leaves, Jesus says to his disciples: "Open your eyes and look at the fields, already ripe."

- They were thinking about lunch.
- He was thinking about harvest.

Discipleship shifts perspective.
It moves from self-concern to Kingdom awareness.
The Samaritan revival begins with one conversation.
Do not underestimate small beginnings.

The Pattern of Discipleship

Let us step back and observe the pattern:

- Curiosity — "What do you want?"
- Invitation — "Come and see."
- Encounter — Identity revealed.
- Transformation — Names changed.
- Witness — "We have found…"
- Expansion — "Open your eyes…"

Discipleship is dynamic.

- It begins personally.
- It grows communally.
- It multiplies missionally.

Call to Response

Jesus still asks: "What do you want?"

He still says: "Come and see."

- He still renames.
- He still satisfies thirst.
- He still opens eyes to harvest.

The question isn't whether the invitation stands.
The question is whether you will respond.

Closing Emphasis

From the beginning, the movement of Jesus spread through personal invitation.

Andrew came—and brought Peter.

Philip came—and brought Nathanael.

A woman came—and brought a village.

Discipleship begins with invitation.

And invitation never ends.

Come and see.

And then go and tell.

Because when you truly see him, you can't help but invite others to see.

The invitation stands.

- Come.
- See.
- Follow.

And watch what he makes of you.

SERMON 5: Authority Like None Other

Theme: Jesus demonstrates divine authority over demons, disease, sin, nature, and religious systems—and calls us to trust and submit fully to him.

Key Texts: Mark 1–2; Matthew 8–9; Luke 4–5

Eyewitness Chapters

"A government official seeks healing for his sick son" to "Two blind men want to see."

Introduction: When Authority Walks into the Room

There is a difference between influence and authority.

- Influence persuades.
  Authority commands.
- Influence suggests.
  Authority decides.
- Influence may be admired.
  Authority must be obeyed.

In our culture, we are skeptical of authority.

- We have seen authority abused.
- We have seen power corrupted.
- We have seen leaders fail.

So when someone claims authority, we instinctively hesitate.

But when Jesus begins his public ministry, something unmistakable happens.

The *Eyewitness* account records the reaction of the crowds: "What powerful new teaching is this? Even the evil spirits obey him."

That statement isn't hyperbole. It's astonishment.

Why?

Because they had never seen authority like this.

- Not borrowed authority.
- Not institutional authority.
- Not inherited authority.

This was authority according to God's nature.

- Authority that didn't appeal to other rabbis.
- Authority that didn't depend on political office.
- Authority that didn't rely on social approval.
- Authority that flowed from who Jesus was.

Today we will walk through several scenes from the early ministry of Jesus and examine what his authority reveals—and what it demands from us.

Because recognizing his authority changes everything.

Authority Over the Invisible Realm

The setting is Capernaum. The synagogue is full. Jesus is teaching.

The *Eyewitness* record says: "People were amazed. The authority with which he spoke was nothing like the teachers of the Law."

Then suddenly, interruption.

A man possessed by an evil spirit screams: "What do you want with us, Jesus of Nazareth? I know who you are, the Holy One sent from God."

Notice something deeply significant.

- Demons recognize what religious leaders debate.
- They know who he is.
- Jesus doesn't argue theology.
- He doesn't engage in discussion.
- He speaks one word: "Silence. Come out of him."

And the spirit obeys.

- Immediately.
- Without negotiation.
- Without delay.

That is authority.

Let us be very clear: Jesus did not appeal to a higher authority.

He did not say, "In someone else's name."

- He spoke as the authority.
- The invisible realm responds to him.
- The powers of darkness recognize him.

The crowd says: "Even the evil spirits obey him."

This is the first public display of his power in Capernaum.

And it reveals something crucial:

- Jesus isn't merely a moral reformer.
- He is sovereign over the spiritual realm.

Many believers fear spiritual darkness.

We fear what we don't see.

But the authority of Jesus establishes something foundational:

- There is no power that rivals him.
- Darkness doesn't share authority.
  It submits to it.

If you belong to Christ, you don't fight *for* victory.

You fight *from* victory.

Authority over the invisible realm belongs to him.

The question isn't whether darkness is real.

The question is whether you trust the One who commands it.

Authority Over Disease

Immediately after the synagogue scene, Jesus enters Peter's house.

Peter's mother-in-law is ill with a severe fever.

The *Eyewitness* text says: "Jesus went to her bedside. As he took her by the hand and helped her sit up, he ordered the fever to go. At once, she got up."

- No incantation.
- No ritual.
- No extended process.
- Authority.

And then, as the sun sets, the entire town gathers.

"When he touched them and spoke a few simple words, he healed each one."

- Each one.
- Not some.
- Not selective.
- Each one.

Isaiah had prophesied: "Truly, he has taken our infirmities and carried our pain."

This isn't random compassion.

This is messianic authority.

- Jesus isn't overwhelmed by sickness.
- He isn't intimidated by disease.
- He doesn't consult charts.
- He commands—and healing follows.

Another scene deepens this revelation.
A leper approaches.

What did it mean when a leper approached?

- Isolation.
- Disgrace.
- Untouchability.

The man says: "Sir, you could make me well if you wanted to."
That statement is remarkable.
He doesn't question ability.
He questions willingness.
Jesus responds: "I want to … Be cleansed."
Authority and compassion meet.
He touches the untouchable.
And the disease disappears.

Authority like no other.

- Authority without compassion is tyranny.
- Compassion without authority is helplessness.

Jesus possesses both. He is willing—and able.
Some of you believe he is able but question his willingness.
Others believe he is willing but question his ability.
This story answers both.
He wants to.
And he can.

Authority Over Sin

Perhaps the most controversial display of authority occurs in a crowded house.

A paralyzed man is lowered through the roof.

Jesus sees their faith and says: "Do not worry, my friend. Your sins are forgiven."

That statement ignites outrage.

The religious leaders think: Only God can forgive sins.

And they are right.

Jesus responds: "Which is easier to say, 'Your sins are forgiven,' or, 'Stand and walk'?"

Then he commands: "Get up. Take your mat and go home."

The man stands.

Healing confirms forgiveness.

Authority over sin is greater than authority over sickness.

Disease affects the body.

Sin affects the soul.

And Jesus addresses both.

Notice something critical:

He forgives before he heals.

Because the deepest paralysis is spiritual, not physical.

Many people seek relief from symptoms but avoid surrendering sin.

Jesus demonstrates that he has authority not only to improve circumstances—but to remove guilt.

If he can command a paralyzed man to walk, he can command your condemnation to leave.

The question is whether you trust his authority to forgive.

Authority Over Religious Systems

Authority like no other also challenges established systems.

- The Pharisees question why his disciples don't fast.
- They question why they pick grain on the Sabbath.
- They question why he heals on the Sabbath.

Jesus replies: "The Sabbath was made to meet the needs of the people, not people to meet the requirements of the Sabbath."

And then: "The Son of Man is Lord even of the Sabbath."

That statement is staggering.
The Sabbath was instituted by God at creation.
And Jesus claims lordship over it.
He doesn't abolish the Law.
He fulfills its purpose.
Authority like no other exposes legalism.
Religion without relationship becomes oppressive.
Jesus restores intention.
Many want Jesus as Savior.
Fewer accept him as Lord.

Authority demands submission.

- If Jesus is Lord of the Sabbath, he is Lord of your schedule.
- If he is Lord of sin, he is Lord of your habits.
- If he is Lord of sickness, he is Lord of your fear.

Authority like none other requires surrender like none other.

Authority Over Calling — "Follow me"

When Jesus passes Matthew, the tax collector, he says: "Follow me."

Matthew leaves everything.
Authority commands allegiance.
Jesus doesn't negotiate.
He doesn't persuade with benefits.
He calls.
And Matthew obeys.
Authority over life direction.
What does Jesus' authority require of you?

Have you acknowledged his authority in:

- Your finances?

- Your relationships?
- Your speech?
- Your ambitions?
- Your private life?

It's possible to admire his power and resist his lordship. But true discipleship submits.

Authority Confirmed by Amazement

Throughout these scenes, a repeated phrase appears:

- "They were amazed."
- "They marveled."
- "We've never seen anything like this before."

Authority produces awe.

Familiarity dulls awe.

If Jesus feels ordinary to you, you may have forgotten who he is.

Authority demands reverence.

Call to Response

Let me ask plainly: Do you trust Jesus' authority?

- When he says, "Come out," darkness leaves.
- When he says, "Be cleansed," disease retreats.
- When he says, "Forgiven," guilt dissolves.
- When he says, "Follow me," destiny changes.

Will you submit?

Closing Emphasis

Authority like none other.

- He commands demons—and they obey.
- He touches disease—and it flees.

- He forgives sin—and condemnation collapses.
- He confronts religion—and restores truth.
- He calls disciples—and they follow.

And the One who holds that authority stretches out his hands—not to dominate—but to redeem.

- Trust him.
- Submit to him.
- Follow him.

Because there has never been—
and never will be—
authority like his.

SERMON 6:
From Glory to the Cross

Theme: The Messiah's path to victory runs through suffering, surrender, and resurrection.

Key Texts: John 12–19; Luke 22–24

Eyewitness Chapters

"Mary anoints Jesus with expensive perfume" to "The disciples watch Jesus ascend into the clouds."

Introduction: The Week that Changed Everything

One week.

Seven days.

A parade on Sunday.

A trial on Friday.

An empty tomb at dawn.

- Some of the voices that shouted, "Hosanna," would soon cry, "Crucify him."
- Some of the hands that waved palm branches would later clench into fists.
- The same city that celebrated him would condemn him.

This final movement in the life of Christ reveals something profoundly important: Glory and suffering are not opposites in God's plan. They are connected.

The path to resurrection runs through a cross.

The *Eyewitness* account reminds us of the prophetic words spoken early in Jesus' life: "This child will cause the rise and fall of many in Israel."

Those words frame the final week.

Jesus doesn't *stumble* into suffering.

He *walks* toward it.

Today we will walk that road carefully—because if we misunderstand the cross, we misunderstand Christianity.

The Triumphal Entry — Glory Misunderstood

Jesus enters Jerusalem riding a donkey.

Crowds line the road.

- They cheer.
- They celebrate.
- They spread garments and branches.
- They expect deliverance.
- They expect revolution.
- They expect political triumph.

But Jesus rides a donkey—not a warhorse.

He fulfills prophecy, but not their expectation.

- They want Rome overthrown.
  He intends for sin to be destroyed.
- They want national restoration.
  He brings spiritual redemption.
- The glory they imagine is immediate power.
  The glory he brings is sacrificial love.

There is a warning here.

It's possible to celebrate Jesus for the wrong reasons.

It's possible to cheer for him while misunderstanding him.

The crowd's enthusiasm is real—but shallow.

When their expectations are not met, their loyalty dissolves.

Why do you follow Jesus?

- For blessing?
- For comfort?
- For success?
- Or for salvation?

If you follow him only for triumph, you will stumble at the cross.

The Upper Room — Servanthood Revealed

Just before the darkest moment in history, Jesus revealed what true greatness looks like.

Before the cross, there is a meal.

Before betrayal, there is bread.

Jesus gathers his disciples.

He does something shocking.

He washes their feet.

The Master kneels.

The Lord serves.

Authority expresses itself through humility.

He tells them: "I have set you an example."

This is the upside-down kingdom.

- Power kneels.
- Greatness serves.
- Glory stoops.

If the King washed feet, no act of service is beneath you.

The cross begins with humility.

Gethsemane — The Battle of Wills

Now, we step into the garden.

This is perhaps the most sacred ground in the Gospel narrative.

Jesus isn't surrounded by crowds.

He isn't performing miracles.

He is praying.

He knows what is coming.

- Betrayal.
- Beating.
- Mockery.
- Crucifixion.

He prays: "Father, if it is possible … not my will, but yours."

This isn't fear of death.

It's submission to divine purpose.

The cross isn't imposed upon him.

It's embraced.

He could call angels.

He could walk away.

He does not.

Victory begins with surrender.

The greatest battles of obedience are fought in private prayer.

Before you face public trials, settle private surrender.

The Arrest and Trial — Innocence Condemned

The road to the cross unfolds with a series of painful and powerful moments.

Judas arrives with soldiers.

A kiss marks betrayal.

Jesus doesn't resist.

Peter draws a sword.

Jesus tells him to put it away.

The Messiah will not be defended by violence.

He is taken.

He stands before Caiaphas.

False witnesses speak.

He remains composed.
He stands before Pilate.
Pilate finds no fault.
Yet fear of the crowd overcomes courage.
The mob shouts for crucifixion.
Barabbas is released.
Jesus is condemned.
The innocent dies for the guilty.
This is substitution.
The cross isn't a tragic accident.
It's divine exchange.
Barabbas walked free because Jesus took his place.
So do we.

The Cross — Glory Through Suffering

Now, we stand at Calvary.
Nails pierce flesh.
Wood supports weight.
Blood falls to dust.

The *Eyewitness* account states plainly: "Jesus is nailed to the cross and dies."

- No embellishment.
- No dramatic exaggeration.
- Just truth.

While enduring pain on the cross, what does he do?

- He prays for forgiveness.
- He promises paradise.
- He entrusts his mother.
- He declares completion.

"It is finished."
What is finished?

- The debt of sin.
- The requirement of sacrifice.
- The barrier between God and humanity.

The Lamb fulfills his purpose.

- Darkness falls.
- The earth trembles.
- The curtain tears.
- Access is opened.

The cross isn't merely an example.

- It's atonement.
- Do not reduce it to symbolism.
- It's substitution.

The Silence of Saturday

Between the sorrow of the cross and the triumph of resurrection lies a quiet, difficult day.

The body is laid in a tomb.
The stone is rolled in place.
Hope appears to be buried.
Disciples scatter.
Fear spreads.
Silence reigns.
Sometimes redemption feels delayed.
Saturday is the day of doubt.
But silence isn't defeat.
God works even when unseen.
If you are in a "Saturday" season—wait.
Resurrection is coming.

The Resurrection — Authority Vindicated

Then the morning came that changed everything.

At dawn, women approach the tomb.

The stone is rolled away.

The body is gone.

Angels announce: "He is risen."

The *Eyewitness* account records: "The tomb is opened, and people can't find Jesus' body."

Jesus appears.

He speaks peace.

He shows scars.

Death is defeated.

Authority is vindicated.

The cross without resurrection is *tragedy*.

The resurrection without the cross is *meaningless*.

Together, they are redemption.

The same power that raised Christ is available to transform you.

Resurrection isn't merely future hope.

It's present reality.

The Ascension — Glory Restored

Finally, the disciples watch Jesus ascend.

He blesses them.

He rises.

Clouds receive him.

Glory returns.

But now—scarred glory.

Heaven holds a Lamb.

Victory through wounds.

The path of Christ defines the path of discipleship.

Glory through surrender.

Life through death.

Exaltation through humility.

Call to Response

The cross confronts every heart.
You can't remain neutral.

- He was rejected.
- He was mocked.
- He was crucified.
- He rose.

Will you reject?
Or will you believe?
The road from glory to the cross was walked for you.
Step into the redemption it purchased.

Closing Emphasis

The road of redemption unfolded step-by-step.
Palm branches fell.
The cross stood.
The tomb closed.
The stone rolled.
The grave emptied.
He rose.
From glory—
To suffering—
To surrender—
To resurrection—
To reigning.
And the same Savior who walked that road invites you to follow him.

Not to avoid the cross—but to trust the One who conquered it.

- He came.
- He died.
- He rose.
- He reigns.

Amen.

From Pulpit to Person: Using Eyewitness as an Evangelism Tool

You have preached the Light. You have proclaimed repentance. You have lifted high the cross. You have declared the resurrection.

Now, the question isn't simply, *What will we teach next?* The question is, "*Who will we reach next?*"

The six sermons have unfolded the life of Christ. But the book *Eyewitness: The Life of Christ Told in One Story* was written with a very specific burden: to help believers share the Gospel with people who will not read the Bible—but who *will* read a story.

That distinction matters. Many unbelievers will never open Matthew, Mark, Luke, or John separately. Some believers see only the Bible verses that are displayed on a screen during a weekend sermon, so they still struggle to see the full picture. Most Christians think they know the story of Jesus—but they can't visualize it as one unified life.

Eyewitness bridges that gap.

It isn't a replacement for Scripture.

It's a doorway into Scripture. After reading *Eyewitness*, many have said, "Now I'm reading the Bible." It arranges the testimony so people can see Jesus clearly—chronologically, cohesively, and compellingly.

If the six sermons stirred your church's heart, now it is time to place an evangelism tool in their hands.

1. From Sermon Series to Evangelism Strategy

These messages were never meant to terminate inside the sanctuary.

They are launching pads.

The structure of the six sermons mirrors the structure of *Eyewitness*:

- The eternal Word.
- Heaven's interruption.
- The call to repentance.
- The Kingdom revealed.
- The cross.
- The resurrection.

That progression isn't just theological. It's evangelistic.

It answers the core questions every human heart asks:

- Who is Jesus?
- Why did he come?
- What did he teach?
- Why did he die?
- Did he rise?
- What does that mean for me?

Your next step is to equip people, not only to understand those answers, but to share them with others.

2. *Eyewitness* Reaches People Who Don't Read the Bible

One of the greatest evangelistic challenges of our time is biblical unfamiliarity.

We are no longer living in a culture where people:

- Know the Gospel narrative.
- Understand biblical language.

- Recognize scriptural sequence.

Many people assume they know the story of Jesus—but actually, they know fragments, and they don't know what they don't know.

- Some know Christmas.
- Some know Easter.
- Few know the whole.

Eyewitness assembles the life of Christ into one continuous narrative so readers can follow him step-by-step. It removes the confusion of flipping between four Gospels. It eliminates the intimidation factor of unfamiliar structure. It presents the story in accessible language without sacrificing theological integrity.

- For believers, it strengthens clarity.
- For seekers, it removes barriers.
- For skeptics, it provides coherence.

It's especially powerful for:

- New believers who feel overwhelmed by Scripture.
- Unchurched friends who are curious about Jesus.
- Family members who are resistant to "religious talk."
- Young adults who prefer narrative over exposition.

The book does what many sermons can't do alone. It places the entire life of Christ into someone's hands.

3. Equip your Church to Share It

Here is one great opportunity: Instead of asking people to invite others to church, invite them to place *Eyewitness* into someone's life.

Imagine encouraging every family in your church to prayerfully identify:

- One coworker.

- One neighbor.
- One family member.
- One spiritually curious friend.

Then all they have to say is: "This book presents the story of Jesus in a way you've never read before. I think you'll love it."

- Not a debate.
- Not a lecture.
- Not a confrontation.
- A story.

People who resist argument often welcome narrative.

You are not asking them to adopt doctrine.

You are asking them to meet a Person.

4. A Tool for Both Believers and Nonbelievers

Church leaders often struggle with this question: "How do I disciple believers and evangelize unbelievers at the same time?"

Eyewitness answers both needs.

For Believers:

- It deepens understanding of chronology.
- It strengthens confidence in testimony.
- It clarifies the unity of Scripture.
- It rekindles awe at the coherence of Christ's life.

When believers see the whole story, their faith stabilizes.

For Nonbelievers:

- It removes the intimidation of multiple books.
- It eliminates confusion about sequence.
- It presents Jesus without denominational noise.

- It invites them to evaluate the life of Christ directly.

It allows the story itself to speak.
And the life of Jesus, when seen clearly, is transformative.

5. Shift the Culture: From Attraction to Activation

Many churches operate primarily in attraction mode:

- "Come hear a sermon."
- "Come to an event."
- "Come to a service."

There is value in gathering. But what if your congregation became carriers of the story? What if every member saw themselves as an eyewitness sharer?

The early church did not rely on buildings. They relied on testimony.

Eyewitness is structured around testimony. It reminds readers that these are not fictional myths but carefully investigated accounts. It echoes the heart of 1 John: "We have seen… we have heard… we have touched…"

When believers internalize that framework, evangelism becomes natural. They are not promoting a program. They are sharing what they have seen.

6. Build Practical Evangelistic Pathways

Consider these next steps:

A. Host Reading Groups

Encourage small groups where believers and seekers read one section of *Eyewitness* per week and discuss:

- What does this reveal about Jesus?
- What surprises you?
- What challenges you?

B. Offer "Meet Jesus" Evenings

Instead of an apologetics debate, host gatherings centered on reading selected passages aloud and discussing them.

C. Give It as a Gift

Equip your church to:

- Give it at Christmas instead of another devotional.
- Give it at Easter as a resurrection-centered gift.
- Give it to graduates.
- Give it to those walking through crisis.

A narrative can enter places where sermons never will.

7. Remember the Goal: Changed Lives

The purpose isn't distribution.

The purpose is transformation.

People's lives change when they encounter:

- The authority of Jesus.
- The compassion of Jesus.
- The sacrifice of Jesus.
- The resurrection of Jesus.

Many unbelievers reject caricatures of Christianity.

Few remain unmoved when confronted with the coherent life of Christ.

When they see:

- The consistency of his teaching,
- The courage of his sacrifice,
- The fulfillment of prophecy,
- The eyewitness testimony of resurrection,

They must respond.

We are called to do more than simply preach about Jesus. It's to introduce people to him. *Eyewitness* helps us do that.

8. A Final Word to Pastors

You have preached the six movements of redemption.

Now, mobilize your people.

Help them see that evangelism is not:

- Winning arguments.
- Mastering techniques.
- Forcing decisions.

It's placing the life of Christ in front of someone and saying: "Read this. See him for yourself."

- Some will reject him.
- Some will wrestle.
- Some will believe.

But none will remain unchanged by an honest encounter. The Light that could not be overcome still shines. The cross still redeems. The resurrection still transforms.

Eyewitness is more than a book.

It's an invitation.

Now, send it out.

Let your church become, not just hearers of the story, but carriers of a life-changing message.

And trust that when people truly see Jesus, lives will be transformed.

Sermons for Special Occasions

1. CHRISTMAS SEASON: The Word Became Flesh

Introduction: The Strangest Claim Ever Made

Every Christmas, we gather around something astonishing.

Not just a baby.

Not just a manger.

But a claim.

A claim so bold that if it isn't true, it is madness.

And if it is true, it changes everything.

At the beginning of the story, we are told:

"The Word became human and lived among his own people."

Not metaphorically.

Not symbolically.

Not spiritually only.

The Word.

Became flesh.

That is Christmas.

Before the Manger — Eternity

Christmas doesn't begin in Bethlehem.

It begins before creation.

- Before shepherds.
- Before angels.
- Before stars.

The story begins in eternity.

Jesus was not *created* in a stable.

He *entered* one.
Christmas isn't the origin of Christ.
It's the arrival of Christ.
And that means:
The baby in the manger isn't merely adorable.
He is eternal.

God Moves Toward Us

When humanity rebelled, God did not retreat.

He moved closer.

Throughout the story, anticipation builds:

A voice in the wilderness.

A promise to Israel.

A longing for redemption.

And then, suddenly, heaven breaks silence.

Angels appear.

Shepherds tremble.

And light pierces the dark.

The birth narrative in *Eyewitness* reminds us that heaven did not whisper.

It declared.

Because salvation had entered history.

Why a Manger?

If you were writing about the arrival of a King, would you choose:

- A borrowed feeding trough?
- A teenage mother?
- A carpenter?
- Shepherds as first witnesses?

Of course not.

But God did.

Why?

Because the Kingdom of God doesn't enter through power.

It enters through humility.

The incarnation is the greatest act of humility ever known.

The Creator entered creation.

The Author stepped into the story.

The Infinite accepted limitation.

Not because he had to.

Because he chose to.

Light in the Darkness

Christmas happens in darkness.

- Politically.
- Spiritually.
- Morally.

Rome ruled with iron.

Religion had become ritual.

Hope was thin.

And into that darkness, light appeared.

Light doesn't argue with darkness.

It overcomes it.

When the Word became flesh, light entered the room.

And darkness has never recovered.

That is why Christmas isn't sentimental.

It's revolutionary.

The Lamb Arrives

Early in the story, John the Baptizer declares: "Look! The Lamb of God, who takes away the sin of the world."

At Christmas, the Lamb arrives.

The cradle already points to the cross.

The wood of the manger anticipates the wood of Calvary.

The tiny hands that grasp Mary's finger will one day be pierced.

This isn't accidental poetry.

It's divine purpose.

The incarnation isn't complete without redemption.

He came to die.

And he came willingly.

God with Us

Christmas isn't primarily about gifts.

It's about presence.

God with us.

- Not distant.
- Not detached.
- Not abstract.

With us.

- In weakness.
- In poverty.
- In obscurity.

If you have ever wondered whether God understands your struggle—

Look at the manger.

- He knows hunger.
- He knows rejection.
- He knows vulnerability.

Christmas declares: You are not alone.

The Decision that Christmas Demands

The arrival of Jesus forced everyone who encountered him to make a choice.

- The shepherds came.

- The Magi bowed.
- Herod raged.

Even at his birth, division appeared.

Christmas forces a decision.

Is he:

- Decoration?
- Tradition?
- Inspiration?

Or is he Lord?

If the Word truly became flesh, then neutrality is impossible.

You either *receive* him.

Or you *resist* him.

Because He Came

The coming of Jesus changed everything.

- Sin can be forgiven.
- Shame can be removed.
- Fear can be silenced.
- Death can be defeated.

The baby in the manger is the King on the throne.

The cradle leads to the cross.

The cross leads to the empty tomb.

And the empty tomb leads to eternal hope.

The Invitation

That night long ago, there was no room in the inn.

But there was room in a stable.

Today, the question isn't whether there was room in Bethlehem.

The question is:

Is there room for him in your heart?

The Word became flesh.
He moved toward us.
Now, we move toward him.
Let us not leave him in the manger.
Let's crown him.

Closing Prayer

Lord Jesus,
You are not merely the child of Christmas.
You are the eternal Word made flesh.
Thank you for coming near.
Thank you for humility.
Thank you for redemption.
And thank you for light that overcomes darkness.
We receive you, not as tradition,
But as Lord.
Amen.

2. LENT (Six Weeks Before Easter): Prepare the Way

Introduction: Lent Is a Journey, Not a Season

Christians have set aside these forty days for a purpose far greater than ritual.

Lent isn't decoration.
It isn't liturgical routine.
It's a journey.

- Forty days of examination.
- Forty days of recalibration.
- Forty days of preparing our hearts.

Before there was a cross, there was a wilderness.
Before resurrection glory, there was desert testing.
Lent invites us into that desert.

A Voice in the Wilderness

Before Jesus begins public ministry, a voice cries out.
A prophet stands in the desert.

- Calling people to repent.
- Calling them to prepare.

The message is simple:
Make the path straight.

In *Eyewitness*, we are reminded that this moment isn't random.

- It's fulfillment.

- It’s preparation.
- It’s a divine interruption of spiritual complacency.

The desert becomes a place of awakening.
Why the wilderness?
Because the wilderness strips away distraction.

- No cities.
- No applause.
- No pretense.

Just honesty.
Lent is spiritual wilderness.
And the question is:
What in your life needs straightening?

Repentance Before Glory

Before the ministry of Jesus began in power, another message had to be heard.

- John the Baptizer’s call isn’t condemnation.
  It’s invitation.
- Repentance isn’t humiliation.
  It’s alignment.

Before Jesus performs miracles…
Before crowds gather…
Before authority is displayed…
There is repentance.
We want victory without surrender.
We want resurrection without confession.
But Lent reminds us:
Preparation precedes power.

Identity Declared Before Performance

The ministry of Jesus begins, not with action, but with affirmation.

At his baptism, heaven opens.
And the Father declares his pleasure.
Approval before achievement.
Identity before action.
This is crucial.
Jesus has done no miracles yet.
He has preached no sermons.
And yet, he is declared *beloved.*

Lent confronts a dangerous lie:
That God loves us because we perform? No.
Obedience flows *from* identity—not *toward* it.

The Wilderness Test

Immediately after baptism, Jesus enters the wilderness.

Not by accident.
By design.
Temptation follows affirmation.
The enemy attacks the declaration:
"If you are the Son of God..."
Notice the strategy.
The attack isn't on ability.
It's on identity.

Three Temptations:

- Turn stones to bread —
  Use power for yourself.
- Jump from the Temple —
  Prove yourself publicly.

- Bow for kingdoms —
  Take glory without the cross.

Each temptation shortcuts suffering.
Each temptation bypasses obedience to the Father.
Each temptation avoids surrender.
Lent is about resisting shortcuts.

The Power of "No"

Jesus responds with Scripture.
Not argument.
Not spectacle.

- He answers temptation with truth.
- He refuses bread without obedience.
- He refuses glory without submission.
- He refuses power without the cross.

Victory in the wilderness makes Calvary possible.

Before he conquers death *publicly*, he conquers temptation *privately*.

What Lent Reveals About Us

Lent asks uncomfortable questions:

- Where are we tempted to shortcut obedience?
- Where do we crave applause?
- Where do we avoid surrender?

The wilderness exposes appetite.
And appetite reveals allegiance.

Preparing for the Cross

The wilderness isn't the end.
It's preparation.

Jesus leaves the desert ready.

- Ready for opposition.
- Ready for misunderstanding.
- Ready for the cross.

And Lent prepares us for Good Friday.

Because the cross cannot be appreciated without confession.

Resurrection cannot be celebrated without surrender.

Personal Application

Let me ask you plainly:

- What appetite needs discipline?
- What identity lie needs correction?
- What shortcut needs refusal?

Lent isn't about giving up chocolate.
It's about giving up self-rule.
It's about straightening the path.

Make the Way Straight

A voice cried in the wilderness:
Prepare the way.
That voice still echoes.
Not in deserts of sand.
But in deserts of distraction.
God doesn't force the path.
He invites us to clear it.
And when the path is straight,
Grace moves freely.

Closing Prayer

Lord Jesus,
As we enter this Lenten journey,

strip away what distracts.
Expose what tempts.
Correct what distorts.
And prepare us for the cross.
Teach us to surrender before glory.
And to resist shortcuts to obedience.
Amen.

3. PALM SUNDAY:
Crown Him or Crucify Him

Introduction: A Parade Like None Other

Jerusalem had seen parades before.

- Roman generals entered with war horses.
- Soldiers marched in formation.
- Banners waved.
- Armor gleamed.
- Power announced itself loudly.

But this parade was different.
"People cheer as Jesus rides into Jerusalem on a donkey."

- No warhorse.
- No sword.
- No army.

A donkey.
And palm branches.
Palm Sunday isn't just celebration.
It's confrontation.
Because the question isn't whether they waved palms.
The question is whether they understood the King.

The King They Wanted

The crowd shouted.
"Hosanna!"
Which means:
Save us now.

But what kind of salvation did they want?

- Political freedom.
- Roman overthrow.
- National restoration.

They wanted a King who would crush their enemies.

And Jesus came to conquer something much more important.

We often want relief from circumstances.

Jesus came to rescue us from sin.

The Donkey Declares Something

Why a donkey?

- Because this was prophecy fulfilled.
- Because this was peace declared.
- Because this King doesn't arrive by force.

He arrives by humility.

Rome entered cities with fear.

Jesus entered with surrender.

The crowd expected revolution.

He brought redemption.

And redemption doesn't always look powerful.

It looks vulnerable.

Easy Praise

Praise is easy when expectations are met.

On Sunday they cried:

"Hosanna!"

By Friday some would cry:

"Crucify him!"

What changed?

Their expectations.

When Jesus didn't overthrow Rome, when he didn't seize political control, when he confronted religious hypocrisy instead of Roman soldiers—

Praise shifted to disappointment.

And disappointment can turn into rejection.

Palm Sunday reminds us:

Public enthusiasm isn't the same as surrendered allegiance.

Authority Challenged

After entering Jerusalem, Jesus doesn't seize a throne.

He confronts leaders.

He speaks in parables that expose hearts.

"Religious leaders question Jesus' authority."

The issue becomes clear.

Not miracle.

Not teaching.

Authority.

Who has the right to rule?

And that question has never disappeared.

The Line Is Drawn

Palm Sunday is the moment the line becomes visible.

The King has entered.

The people must decide.

- Crown him.
- Or crucify him.

There is no neutral ground.

The city buzzes.

The leaders plot.

The crowd wavers.

And Jesus moves steadily toward the cross.

- Not surprised.

- Not trapped.
- Not confused.

He knows exactly what this parade will cost him.

The Irony of the Palm

Jerusalem welcomed a king—but misunderstood the kind of victory he came to bring.

Palms symbolized victory.

But the victory would not look like anyone expected.

- Not military triumph.
  But sacrificial love.
- Not domination.
  But crucifixion.

The same city that welcomed him would reject him.

And yet he entered anyway.

Why?

- Because love moves toward betrayal.
- Because obedience moves toward suffering.
- Because redemption requires sacrifice.

The Question for Us

Celebrating Jesus is easy, but following him is costly.

- It's easy to wave palms.
  It's harder to carry a cross.
- It's easy to sing praise.
  It's harder to surrender control.

So let me ask plainly:

- Do you want the King who meets your expectations?
  Or the King who transforms your heart?

- Do you want comfort?
  Or do you want salvation?

Because the King on a donkey is also the Lamb on a cross. And the cross isn't optional in his Kingdom.

The Coming Week

Palm Sunday isn't the conclusion of the story. It's the doorway into the drama of Holy Week.

- Celebration turns to confrontation.
- Cheers turn to betrayal.
- Hosanna turns to crucify.

But here is the deeper truth:

The King who entered Jerusalem humbly will one day return in glory.

- The first entry was on a donkey.
  The next will not be.
- The first entry brought redemption.
  The next will bring restoration.

Crown Him

Palm Sunday forces a decision.

Not about palm branches.
About allegiance.
The crowd shouted.
But only a few stayed faithful.
Will we crown him only when he blesses us?
Or will we crown him when he challenges us?
He entered the city knowing the cross awaited him.
He entered because he loves.
And today, the invitation stands:
Crown him.
Not with branches.

With your life.

Closing Prayer

Lord Jesus,
You entered Jerusalem in humility,
knowing the cross was ahead.
Forgive us when we praise you for comfort.
but resist you in surrender.
Teach us to crown you fully—
not just with words,
but with obedience.
Amen.

4. MAUNDY THURSDAY:
The Table Before the Cross

Introduction: The Quiet Before the Storm

Palm Sunday was public celebration. Maundy Thursday is private revelation.

Palm branches are gone.

The cheers have faded.

The city is tense.

And Jesus gathers his disciples for a meal.

- Not a rally.
- Not a miracle.
- A table.

"Jesus celebrates Passover with the disciples."

Maundy Thursday is quieter than Palm Sunday.

But it may be more revealing.

Because here, before the cross, Jesus explains what the cross means.

Passover Rewritten

Passover was Israel's story.

- Slavery.
- Judgment.
- A lamb's blood on the door.
- Deliverance from death.

For generations, this meal remembered rescue from Egypt.

But now, at this table, Jesus does something astonishing.

He takes bread.
He takes the cup.
And he reframes the story around himself.
The Lamb of Exodus becomes the Lamb of God.
This isn't symbolism alone.
It's fulfillment.
Earlier in the narrative, John declared: "Look! The Lamb of God, who takes away the sin of the world."
Now, that Lamb sits at the table.
And within hours, he will be offered.

A Table with Betrayal

This meal isn't sentimental.
It includes a traitor.
Judas sits close enough to dip bread in the same bowl.
Imagine the tension.
Jesus knows.
Judas knows.
And yet Jesus doesn't explode in anger.
He serves.
Maundy Thursday reminds us:
The love of Christ extends even toward betrayal.
The table isn't built for the deserving.
It's built for the broken.

A New Covenant

Jesus takes the cup and declares it a covenant.
A covenant sealed in blood.

- The old covenant was written on stone.
  The new covenant would be written on hearts.
- The old covenant required repeated sacrifice.
  The new covenant would be secured by one.

Forever.

The cross isn't an accident.
It's agreement.
A divine promise fulfilled in human flesh.

Humility Before Sacrifice

In this same evening, Jesus kneels.
He washes feet.
The King bends.
The Master serves.
The One who will bear the sins of the world stoops to clean dust.
Why?
Because love isn't abstract.
It's embodied.
Maundy means "mandate."
The command given that night:
Love one another.
Not sentimentally.
Sacrificially.
The towel precedes the cross.
Service precedes sacrifice.

The Shadow of Gethsemane

What begins with bread and wine will soon lead to prayer, anguish, and surrender.
After the meal comes the garden.
After the bread comes the cup of suffering.
"Jesus prays at Gethsemane."
The cup of communion becomes the cup of wrath.
He prays in anguish.
He sweats in surrender.
Yet he says yes.
The table prepares him for the garden.
The meal strengthens him for the cross.

What This Means for Us

Maundy Thursday asks three questions:

- Will you receive the covenant?
- Will you embody the command?
- Will you remain when others scatter?

The disciples will falter.
Peter will deny.
Judas will betray.
But the covenant will hold.
Because its strength doesn't depend on human loyalty.
It depends on divine faithfulness.

Communion Reflection

When we take the bread and cup, we are not reenacting nostalgia.

We are proclaiming:

- The Lamb has been given.
- The covenant stands.
- The sacrifice was sufficient.

We do not come to this table because we are worthy.
We come because *he* is.

The Table Still Stands

The table in the upper room has long been cleared.

But the invitation remains.

- Come.
- Receive grace.
- Accept the covenant.
- Live the command.

And remember:

The table comes before the cross.
But the cross fulfills the table.

Communion Prayer

Lord Jesus,
On the night you were betrayed,
You gave thanks.
You broke bread.
You poured the cup.
You gave yourself.
Now, we remember.
Now, we receive.
Now, we commit to love as you loved us.
Amen.

5. GOOD FRIDAY:
Not an Accident

Introduction: The Darkest Day

We call it Good Friday.

But nothing about it appears good.

- Betrayal.
- False accusation.
- Mockery.
- Violence.
- A cross.

The sky darkens.
The crowd jeers.
The disciples scatter.
And at the center stands a man condemned.
"Jesus is nailed to the cross and dies."
But this wasn't chaos.
It wasn't miscalculation.
It wasn't a failed revolution.
It *was* the plan.

Silence of the Lamb

Before the cross, there were trials.

Jesus is tried before Caiaphas.
Jesus stands before Pilate.
False witnesses speak.
Crowds shout.

Pilate hesitates.

And Jesus remains largely silent.

Why?

Because the Lamb doesn't argue.

Earlier in the story, John declared: "Look! The Lamb of God, who takes away the sin of the world."

- Lambs don't defend themselves.
  They are offered.
- Jesus' silence was not weakness.
  It was willingness.

The Exchange

Before the cross is even raised, the meaning of the cross is already on display.

Criminals are released.

Barabbas walks free.

Jesus takes his place.

The innocent condemned.

The guilty released.

This is the exchange.

And it isn't only Barabbas.

It's us, as well.

The cross is substitution.

Not symbol.

Not tragedy.

Substitution.

He stands where we should stand.

He bears what we should bear.

The Weight of Sin

The cross has become a symbol of faith—but in the first century it was an instrument of terror.

Crucifixion was brutal.

Public humiliation.
Slow suffocation.
Agonizing exposure.

- The One who calmed storms now struggles for breath.
- The One who fed thousands is thirsty.
- The One who healed is wounded.

And beyond physical agony lies something deeper:
The weight of sin.
Not his sin.
Ours.
Every lie.
Every act of pride.
Every hidden bitterness.
Every betrayal.
Laid upon him.

The Cry

At the cross, Jesus cries out.

A cry of abandonment.

A cry from the depth of suffering.

This isn't theatrical.

It's real.

The Son who had known eternal communion now experiences separation.

So that we would never have to.

Good Friday reveals both the horror of sin and the holiness of God.

And yet it reveals something greater:

Love.

The Veil Torn

As Jesus breathes his last, something happens.

The earth shakes.

The Temple veil is ripped apart.
Access is opened.
The barrier falls.
The separation is removed.
The cross isn't defeat.
It's access.
The cross isn't loss.
It's victory concealed in suffering.

Why It Had to Be This Way

Why not another way?

- Because justice demands satisfaction.
- Because love requires sacrifice.
- Because redemption costs something.

The manger pointed here.
The Lamb was born to be offered.
And he came willingly.
No one forced him.
No one surprised him.
He walked toward Jerusalem knowing this moment would come.
Palm branches would become thorns.
Hosannas would become insults.
And still he came.

What This Means for Us

Good Friday leaves no room for casual faith.
The cross demands response.
You cannot look at Calvary and remain neutral.
The cross says:

- You are more sinful than you thought.
- And more loved than you can imagine.

The question isn't whether Christ died.
The question is whether we receive what he purchased.

Stay at the Cross

Resist the urge to rush to Sunday.
Sit here.
Feel the weight.
See the cost.
Because resurrection shines brightest when we understand crucifixion.
The cross isn't decorative.
It's decisive.

The Sacrificial Lamb

Today, we don't celebrate loudly.
We remember reverently.
The Lamb was given.
The debt was paid.
The sacrifice was complete.
And although the sky darkened,
Hope was not extinguished.
Because what looked like defeat was redemption unfolding.

Closing Prayer

Lord Jesus,
You bore what we deserved.
You stood where we should have stood.
Forgive us for minimizing the cross.
Teach us to see both the cost and the love.
We bow before the Lamb who was slain.
Amen.

6. EASTER SUNDAY: The Stone Was Not the End

Introduction: Everything Looked Hopeless

Friday ended in darkness.

- The sky blackened.
- The earth shook.
- The Lamb was slain.

"Jesus is nailed to the cross and dies."
Hope seemed buried.
A stone sealed the tomb.
Guards stood watch.
Disciples hid in fear.
From every human perspective, it was over.
But heaven was not finished.

Silence of Saturday

There is something haunting about Saturday.

- No miracles.
- No angels singing.
- No public declarations.

Just silence.
The disciples replayed every word.
Every promise.
Every miracle.
And wondered how it ended in a tomb.
Have you ever lived in a Saturday?

- Between promise and fulfillment.
- Between prayer and answer.
- Between loss and restoration.

Saturday teaches us something:
God is still working when we cannot see it.

The Empty Tomb

Then comes Sunday.

The tomb is opened, and people can't find Jesus' body.
The stone is moved.
Not to let Jesus out.
But to let witnesses in.
Notice something important:
The resurrection was not immediately understood.
There was confusion.

- Fear.
- Running.
- Questions.

Resurrection disrupts assumptions.
It shatters finality.

The stone they thought ended the story became the doorway to a new beginning.

Why the Resurrection Matters

Time and tradition have softened our view of the cross.

- If Jesus had only died, he would be remembered. But not worshiped.
- If Jesus had only taught, he would be admired. But not obeyed.

The resurrection validates everything:

- His authority.
- His identity.

- His sacrifice.

Without resurrection, the cross is tragedy.

With resurrection, the cross is triumph.

The Road to Emmaus

Two disciples walk away from Jerusalem.

Defeated.

Disillusioned.

Certain it was over.

"Jesus appears to two of his followers on the way to Emmaus."

He walks beside them.

Unrecognized.

Explaining Scripture.

Opening their understanding.

Sometimes Jesus is closer than we perceive.

Recognition comes through revelation.

And when they finally recognize him—

Everything changes.

Despair turns to urgency.

They run back.

Hope cannot stay silent.

Fear Turns to Courage

When Jesus appears to the disciples:

Jesus appears to his disciples for the first time.

These are not bold heroes.

They are hiding.

But resurrection changes men.

Peter, who denied him, will preach him.

Thomas, who doubted, will worship him.

The resurrection did not comfort them into safety.

It launched them into mission.

Why?

Because if death is defeated, fear loses its grip.

What Changed

The empty tomb did more than end a story.
It began a transformation.
The tomb was empty.
The body was gone.
The grave was conquered.
But something else changed.
The disciples stopped hiding.
Cowards became witnesses.
Fearful men became martyrs.
People don't die for what they know is false.
They die for what they have seen.
Resurrection isn't myth.
It's movement.

The Ascended King

The story doesn't end with appearances.
It ends with ascension.
The disciples watch Jesus ascend into the clouds.
The risen Christ isn't merely alive.
He reigns.
The crucified Lamb is the exalted King.
Easter isn't only about empty tombs.
It's about enthroned authority.

What This Means for You

Because he lives:

- Sin doesn't have the final word.
- Shame doesn't define you.
- Death isn't permanent.
- Fear isn't ultimate.

Resurrection isn't abstract theology.
It's personal hope.

- It means your worst failure isn't final.
- It means your darkest Friday has a coming Sunday.
- It means the stone in front of your situation may not be the end.

The Decision

On Friday, the question was:
Will you stay at the cross?
On Sunday, the question is:
Will you believe the resurrection?
You cannot celebrate Easter and remain unchanged.
The empty tomb demands a response.
If Christ is risen—he is Lord.
If he is Lord—we follow.

The Stone Was Not the End

For a moment, it seemed that death had the final word.

- The stone was heavy.
- The silence was long.
- The grief was real.

But the grave couldn't hold him.
The Lamb who was slain lives.
The King who was mocked reigns.
The stone was not the end.
It was the beginning.
He is risen.
And because he lives…
We live.

Closing Prayer

Lord Jesus,

You conquered what we couldn't conquer.
You rose where we would have remained.
Teach us to live in resurrection courage.
Transform fear into faith.
And make us witnesses of the risen King.
Amen.

7. ASCENSION SUNDAY: Why Jesus Had to Leave

Introduction: The Strange Ending

Among the great events of the gospel story, the Ascension is often the most overlooked.

We love Christmas.
We celebrate Easter.
But Ascension?
It feels almost like an interruption.

- After the resurrection appearances…
- After the joy…
- After fear turns to courage…

Jesus leaves.

The disciples watch Jesus ascend into the clouds.
And we might wonder:

- Why leave at all?
- Wouldn't it be easier if he stayed?
- Wouldn't the Church be stronger if Jesus physically walked among us?

But ascension isn't absence.
It's enthronement.

The Work Was Finished

The ascension is the victory lap of redemption.
Jesus did not ascend in defeat.

He ascended in completion.
The cross accomplished redemption.
The resurrection validated victory.
Nothing remained unfinished.
He didn't leave because he was forced.
He left because the mission was accomplished.
Ascension declares:

- The sacrifice was sufficient.
- The debt was paid.
- The victory was secured.

From Savior to King

Each moment of the Gospel reveals another dimension of who Jesus is.

- At the cross, he was the Lamb.
- At the resurrection, he was the Victor.
- At the ascension, he is the King.

Ascension is coronation.
It's the moment the crucified Christ is publicly enthroned.
The disciples are not watching disappearance.
They are witnessing exaltation.
He doesn't retreat.
He reigns.

Why He Had to Leave

Let's answer the tension honestly.

Why leave?

Because if Jesus remained physically present in one place, his presence would be limited to one location.

But through the Spirit, his presence fills the world.

If he stayed beside his disciples, they might cling to dependence.

But in ascending, he commissions them into mission.
If he remained visible, faith would shrink into sight.
But now we walk by trust.
Ascension transforms followers into witnesses.

Shift from Spectator to Being Sent

Notice something profound.

Throughout the Gospels, the disciples watch Jesus.

Now, after ascension, the world will watch the disciple.

The responsibility shifts.

No longer: "Jesus will fix it."

Now: "You go."

Ascension means:

The Church becomes the visible expression of the invisible King.

- The hands that healed are now our hands.
- The voice that proclaimed is now our voice.
- The compassion that moved him must move us.

He Reigns Now

Ascension isn't waiting for a future kingdom.

It's declaring a present one.

Christ isn't merely risen.

He is ruling.

Right now.

- Over history.
- Over nations.
- Over time.

Even when the world looks chaotic, ascension reminds us:

- The throne is occupied.
- The King isn't absent.
- He is sovereign.

The Promise of Return

When Jesus ascends, there is also promise.

The same Jesus who rose will return.

- The first coming was humility.
  The next will be glory.
- The first arrival was on a donkey.
  The next will not be.

Ascension gives the Church hope.
History isn't random.
It's moving toward restoration.

What Ascension Means for Us

Because he ascended:

- We have access to the Father.
- We have authority in his name.
- We have purpose in his mission.
- We have confidence in his reign.

Ascension isn't loss.
It isn't departure.

- It's empowerment.
- It's expansion.

He left one place so he could be present in every place.

The Question

On Easter, the question was:

Do you believe Jesus is alive?
On Ascension Sunday, the question is:
Do you believe Jesus is Lord?
Because if he reigns, we obey.

- If he reigns, we trust.
- If he reigns, we go.

From Eyewitness to Witness

The ascension transforms spectators into messengers.

The disciples began as eyewitnesses.

They end as witnesses.

The cloud doesn't close the story.

It opens the Church age.

The same Christ who walked among them now rules above them and works through them.

Ascension isn't *goodbye.*

It is *go.*

Closing Prayer

Lord Jesus,

You did not leave in defeat.

You ascended in glory.

Teach us to live under your reign.

Send us as witnesses.

And anchor our hope in your promised return.

Amen.

8. PENTECOST: When the Fire Fell

Introduction: From Waiting to Power

Between the promise of Jesus and the power of Pentecost lies a quiet moment of waiting.

After the resurrection, everything changed.
After the ascension, everything shifted.
The disciples watch Jesus ascend into the clouds.
He leaves.
But he promises.
And then they wait.
Pentecost begins, not with noise, but with obedience.
They didn't scatter.
They didn't strategize.
They waited.
And heaven responded.

Why Waiting Matters

Before the power of Pentecost arrived, the disciples had to learn the difficult discipline of waiting.

We don't like waiting.

- We like momentum.
- We like clarity.
- We like action.

But waiting produces dependence.

The disciples had seen:

- The cross.
- The empty tomb.
- The risen Christ.
- The ascended King.

But they were not yet ready to move.
Because power had not yet come.
Resurrection gives hope.
Ascension gives authority.
Pentecost gives power.

The Sound from Heaven

What God had promised through the prophets now arrives with power.

Suddenly, a sound.
Like wind.
Tongues of fire.
The Spirit descends.

- The same Spirit who overshadowed Mary.
- The same Spirit who descended at baptism.
- The same Spirit who raised Christ from the dead.

The Spirit now fills the Church.
This isn't symbolic enthusiasm.
This is divine indwelling.
The Spirit who once rested on prophets now rests on people.
Not one.
All.

Fear Turns into Boldness

Something dramatic happens when the Spirit of God fills ordinary people.

Before Pentecost:

- They hid.
- They locked doors.
- They whispered.

After Pentecost:

- They preach.
- They proclaim.
- They stand publicly.

The same Peter who denied Christ now declares him.

What changed?

Not personality.

Power.

Pentecost transforms timid believers into courageous witnesses.

The Reversal of Babel

What was fractured in Genesis begins to be restored in Acts.

At Babel, languages divided humanity.

At Pentecost, languages unite humanity.

The Gospel is heard by all.

God isn't building one ethnic kingdom.

The Spirit is building a global Church.

Fire rests on each believer.

Not hierarchy.

Not celebrity.

Shared empowerment.

Pentecost is democratized grace.

Birth of the Church

What began with a small group of disciples now becomes a movement that will reach the world.

Pentecost isn't a side note.
It's the birth of the Church.
The risen Christ now works through his people.
The ascended King now reigns through surrendered lives.
The Spirit ignites mission.
The Church doesn't exist for comfort.
It exists for witness.

What the Fire Represents

Throughout Scripture, fire often marks the powerful presence of God.

- Fire purifies.
- Fire illuminates.
- Fire consumes.
- Fire spreads.

The Spirit does the same.

- He purifies the heart.
- He illuminates truth.
- He consumes pride.
- He spreads mission.

Pentecost isn't about emotional intensity.
It's about divine empowerment.

What Pentecost Means for Us

Because of Pentecost:

- We are not alone.
- We are not powerless.

- We are not spectators.

The Spirit who raised Christ from the dead lives within believers.

The mission of Jesus did not end at ascension.

It multiplied at Pentecost.

The Church isn't a memorial society.

It's a Spirit-filled movement.

The Question

Pentecost is the moment when surrendered hearts become instruments of God's mission.

The Spirit has come.

But are we yielded?

Fire falls where surrender exists.

Power flows where obedience remains.

Pentecost asks:

- Are we willing to be sent?
- Are we willing to speak?
- Are we willing to trust?

Because the Spirit doesn't fill for comfort.

He fills for mission.

The Fire Still Falls

Pentecost didn't end when the flames faded from sight. That day began a Spirit-empowered movement that continues wherever hearts remain open to God.

- The wind was real.
- The fire was visible.
- The boldness was undeniable.

Pentecost was not a one-day event.

It was the beginning of an age.

- The risen Christ reigns.
- The Spirit empowers.
- The Church proclaims.
- The fire still falls.

The question isn't whether the Spirit is available.
The question is whether we are open.

Closing Prayer

Holy Spirit,
Fall afresh.
Burn away fear.
Ignite boldness.
Purify motives.
Empower witness.
Make us, not only believers, but proclaimers.
Amen.

9. MISSIONS SUNDAY: Sent with Authority

Introduction: The Church Is More than a Gathering

We gather every week.

- We worship.
- We pray.
- We learn.

But the Church doesn't exist merely to *gather*.

It exists to *go*.

From the beginning of his ministry, Jesus did not build spectators.

He built senders.

He built sent ones.

At one point in the narrative, we read: "Jesus sends another seventy-two disciples into the fields of ministry."

- Not only does he heal.
  He multiplies.
- Not only does he teach.
  He commissions.

Missions isn't a department of the Church.

It's the *identity* of the Church.

The Heart of God Has Always Been Global

Before there was Israel, there was a promise to Abraham:

Through you, all nations will be blessed.

When angels announced Christ's birth, it was good news for all people.

When John pointed to Jesus, he declared: "Look! The Lamb of God, who takes away the sin of the world."

- Not one tribe.
- Not one language.
- Not one culture.

The world.

From the beginning, the Gospel has global intent.

Jesus Sends Ordinary People

Notice something powerful.

- He did not send scholars only.
- He did not send priests only.
- He sent fishermen.
- He sent tax collectors.
- He sent common men and women.

The seventy-two were not elite clergy.

They were disciples.

Which means:

Missions is for followers, not professionals.

He sends them two by two.

- Not alone.
- Not isolated.
- But together.

Mission thrives in community.

Sent with Authority

Jesus did not send people empty-handed.

He gave them authority.

- Authority over fear.
- Authority over darkness.
- Authority to proclaim.

The authority did not originate in them.
It flowed from him.
The same is true today.
We don't go because we are strong.
We go because he reigns.
After resurrection and ascension:
The disciples watch Jesus ascend into the clouds.
Ascension means the King reigns.
Pentecost means the Spirit empowers.
Therefore, we go.
Not timidly.
But confidently.

The Harvest Is Ready

Jesus once said the fields are ready for harvest.
The problem isn't opportunity.
It's laborers.

Look around our world:

- Billions without clear Gospel access.
- Cities filled with spiritual confusion.
- Neighborhoods isolated and searching.

The mission field isn't only overseas.
It's across the street.
The call isn't always to cross an ocean.
Sometimes it's to cross a room.

Obstacles to Mission

Why do we hesitate?

- Fear of rejection.
- Fear of inadequacy.
- Fear of inconvenience.

But the disciples also faced fear.

- Persecution.
- Rejection.
- Misunderstanding.

And yet they went.
Because resurrection courage replaces self-preservation.
When you know death is defeated, risk looks different.

Missions Isn't Optional

Jesus left his followers, not with a suggestion, but with a clear command that would define the very purpose and vitality of the Church.

Jesus did not *suggest* going.

He *commanded* it.

The Church is either a sending movement, or it becomes a settling institution.

When mission fades, maintenance rises.

But when mission burns, the Church lives.

We are not custodians of comfort.

We are carriers of hope.

What Missions Looks Like Today

Missions looks like:

- Supporting global partners.
- Training local leaders.

- Serving the marginalized.
- Planting churches.
- Sharing your testimony.
- Funding the work.
- Praying consistently.
- Going personally.

Some are called to go far.
All are called to go somewhere.

The Cost and the Reward

Mission always demands something from us, but the sacrifice is far outweighed by the eternal joy and impact it produces.

Mission costs time.

- Energy.
- Comfort.
- Sometimes safety.

But the reward?

- Changed lives.
- Eternal impact.
- And the joy of obedience.

When the seventy-two returned, they rejoiced.
Mission produces joy because it aligns us with God's heart.

The Question for Us

The Gospel calls every believer to move from comfortable spectatorship to courageous participation.

- Are we consumers of Christianity?
  Or participants in it?

- Are we moved by the lostness of the world?
  Or comfortable in our circle?

Missions Sunday isn't about a program.
It's about a posture.
Will we be sent?

From Eyewitness to Witness

What began with a handful of men who simply watched the works of Jesus became a movement of people sent to carry his message to the world.

The disciples began as eyewitnesses.
They became witnesses.

The same Christ who walked among them now reigns above us and works through us.

The Spirit empowers.
The King commands.
The harvest waits.
We are sent.

Closing Prayer

Lord Jesus,
You did not save us to keep us stationary.
You sent your disciples, and you send us.
Break our comfort.
Expand our vision.
Ignite our courage.
And make this church a *sending* church.
Amen.

10. COMMUNION EMPHASIS SUNDAY: Remembering What It Cost

Introduction: We Forget Quickly

Because memory fades and gratitude weakens, God gave his people sacred moments that call them back to remember what he has done.

Human beings forget.

- We forget kindnesses.
- We forget promises.
- We forget deliverance.

That is why God builds remembrance into worship.
Before there was a cross, there was a table.
Jesus celebrates Passover with the disciples.
And at that table, he redefined everything.
Communion isn't *routine.*
It is *remembrance.*

Passover and the Pattern of Rescue

For generations, Israel remembered a night in Egypt.

- A lamb slain.
- Blood on doorposts.
- Judgment passing over.

That meal was about rescue.

But in the upper room, Jesus takes that story and points to himself.

The pattern becomes personal.

Earlier in the narrative, John declares:

"Look! The Lamb of God, who takes away the sin of the world."

At the table, the Lamb sits among them.

Within hours, he will be offered.

Communion connects Exodus to Calvary.

This Is My Body

When Jesus takes the bread, he doesn't say, "This represents."

He says, "This is my body."

Broken.

Not accidentally.

Intentionally.

- The body that healed lepers.
- The hands that touched the blind.
- The feet that walked on water.

Broken.

Communion confronts us with the cost of grace.

Grace is free to us.

It was not free to him.

This Is My Blood

Jesus filled an ordinary cup with eternal meaning—pointing forward to the sacrifice that would forever seal God's covenant with his people.

He lifts the cup.

The cup of covenant.

The cup of sacrifice.

The Old Covenant required repeated offerings.

This one would not.

The cross would not be partial.

It would be complete.

When we drink, we proclaim:

- The debt is paid.
- The sacrifice is sufficient.
- The covenant stands.

A Table with Broken People

Look around that upper room.

- Peter will deny.
- Thomas will doubt.
- Judas will betray.

Yet Jesus serves them.
Communion isn't for the flawless.
It's for the forgiven.
We don't come because we are worthy.
We come because he is merciful.

But we do come carefully.

- We examine ourselves.
- We confess honestly.
- We approach reverently.

Remembrance Isn't Nostalgia

When Jesus says "remember," he doesn't mean for us to recall sentimentally.
He wants us to proclaim actively.
Communion is declaration.

Every time we eat and drink, we say:

- The cross still matters.
- The Lamb still reigns.
- The covenant still holds.

It's past event and present reality.

The Cross and Unity

Communion is also communal.

- One bread.
- One cup.
- One body.

The cross removes barriers.

- Ethnic.
- Economic.
- Social.
- Personal.

The same blood that covers me covers you.
We stand level at the table.
There is no hierarchy at Calvary.

Examine Your Heart

Before we take communion, ask:

- Is there sin I have ignored?
- Is there bitterness I have protected?
- Is there pride I have justified?

The cross invites honesty.
Not perfection.
But repentance.

What Communion Declares to the World

When the church gathers around the table, it preaches.
It declares that sacrifice is stronger than violence.
That forgiveness is stronger than shame.
That love is stronger than sin.

Communion is quiet—but it is powerful.

Come to the Table

Communion invites us to pause and approach the table with reverence, remembering the costly love that made our redemption possible.

The table is set.
The Lamb has been given.
The covenant stands.
Do not come casually.
Do not come distracted.
Come grateful.
Come surrendered.
Come remembering what it cost.

Transition to the Elements

As we take the bread, remember his body broken for you.

As we take the cup, remember his blood poured out for you.

Receive not merely bread and juice—
Receive grace.

Closing Prayer

Lord Jesus,
Thank you for the cross.
Thank you for the covenant.
Thank you for the Lamb given.
Examine our hearts.
Cleanse what needs cleansing.
Unify what needs healing.
And help us never treat lightly what cost you everything.
Amen.

11. CHRIST THE KING SUNDAY: The Throne Isn't Empty

Introduction: Who Really Rules

Look at our world.

- Nations rise and fall.
- Elections shift power.
- Markets fluctuate.
- Wars erupt.

History often feels chaotic.
Like no one is really in control.
But Christ the King Sunday declares something bold:

- The throne isn't empty.
- The crucified Lamb reigns.

A King Unlike Any Other

When Jesus entered Jerusalem:
People cheer as Jesus rides into Jerusalem on a donkey.
Not on a warhorse.
Not with an army.
On a donkey.
From the beginning, his kingship defied expectation.
He did not seize power.
He embodied humility.
The world defines kings by dominance.
Jesus defines kingship by sacrifice.

Authority Challenged

Throughout Jesus' ministry, leaders questioned him.

"Religious leaders question Jesus' authority."

The issue was never merely miracles.

It was authority.

Who has the right to rule?

That question hasn't changed.

We still resist authority.

We prefer autonomy.

But Christ did not come merely to inspire.

He came to reign.

The Cross Was a Coronation

Pilate placed a sign above Jesus' head: King of the Jews.

Mockery to some.

But also, truth to others.

The crown of thorns was cruel irony.

Yet in God's design, the cross became the throne.

The King rules, not by crushing enemies, but by conquering sin.

The cross wasn't defeat.

It was enthronement through sacrifice.

The Resurrected King

If Jesus had remained in the tomb, he would have been remembered.

But not worshiped.

The resurrection changed everything.

The tomb is opened, and people can't find Jesus' body.

Death couldn't hold the King.

Authority was validated.

Power was displayed.

Hope was secured.

The Ascended King

And then:

The disciples watch Jesus ascend into the clouds.
Ascension is coronation.
It isn't departure.
It's declaration.
The crucified Christ now reigns over all.
Not someday.
Now.
The throne is occupied.

The King Who Judges

Christ the King Sunday also reminds us:

A reigning King judges.
In his teaching, Jesus spoke of final separation.
Sheep and goats.
Faithfulness evaluated.
Compassion revealed.
Kingly authority includes justice.
This is sobering.
But it is also hopeful.
Because injustice will not have the last word.

- The King sees.
- The King knows.
- The King will set things right.

What His Kingship Means for Us

If Christ is King:

We are not ultimate.

- Our preferences are not ultimate.
- Our culture isn't ultimate.
- Our comfort isn't ultimate.

His reign demands allegiance.
Not partial.
Total.
He isn't Savior only.
He is Lord.

The Different Kingdom

Jesus' Kingdom is marked by:

- Humility over pride.
- Service over domination.
- Forgiveness over revenge.
- Truth over manipulation.

When we pray, "Your Kingdom come," we invite his reign into our lives.

Christ the King Sunday isn't merely theological.
It's personal.
Does he reign in you?

The Promise of Jesus' Return

One day, the whole world will recognize the King it once overlooked.

The King who ascended will return.

- The first coming was in humility.
  The next will be in glory.
- The first arrival was veiled.
  The next will be visible.

Every knee will bow.
Every tongue will confess.
Not because of force.
Because of truth revealed.

Crown Him

We live in the waiting space between Christ's coronation and his visible return...

Between promise and fulfillment.
Between coronation and consummation.
The throne isn't empty.
The King isn't absent.
He reigns.
The question isn't whether he is King.
The question is whether we have crowned him.

- Not with words.
  With obedience.
- Not with sentiment.
  With surrender.

Crown him.

Closing Prayer

Lord Jesus,

You are not only our Savior—
You are our King.
Forgive us where we resist your reign.
Align our hearts with your Kingdom.
Help us live under your authority until the day you return in glory.
Amen.

12. GRADUATION SERVICES: Follow Me

Introduction: A Moment of Transition

Graduation is a threshold.

One chapter closes.

Another opens.

Caps are tossed.

Photos are taken.

Speeches are given.

But beneath the celebration lies a deeper question:

Where do we go from here?

Today isn't merely a ceremony.

It's a commissioning.

Before Jesus sent anyone to preach, before he empowered anyone to heal, he did something simple:

He called them.

The Call Was Personal

At the beginning of his ministry, Jesus approached ordinary people.

Fishermen mending nets.

A tax collector at a booth.

And he said two words:

"Follow me."

Not:

- Understand everything.

- Have it all figured out.
- Be fully qualified.

"Follow me."

The call was personal…

- Before it was public.
- Before it was professional.
- Before it was impressive.

Graduates, hear this clearly:

Your degree doesn't define your ultimate direction.

Your calling does.

He Calls the Unlikely

Jesus built his mission on willing hearts ready to be sent, not on impressive credentials.

The first disciples were not religious elites.

- Ordinary.
- Flawed.
- Imperfect.

Yet Jesus entrusted them with extraordinary mission.

Later in the narrative we see:

"Jesus sends another seventy-two disciples into the fields of ministry."

He multiplies the mission.

He sends not the famous but the faithful.

Graduation often tempts us to measure worth by achievement.

Jesus measures by availability.

Authority Flows from Jesus

When Jesus sent his disciples, he didn't send them alone.

He gives authority.

- Authority over fear.
- Authority over darkness.
- Authority to proclaim.

After resurrection and ascension:

The disciples watch Jesus ascend into the clouds.

Ascension means Christ reigns.

And if he reigns, then the One who sends you has all authority.

Graduates, you will step into classrooms, offices, hospitals, workshops, homes, cities, and nations.

You don't go in your own strength.

You go under his authority.

Count the Cost

Jesus also spoke honestly.

Following him isn't always easy.

There is a cost.

- Rejection.
- Misunderstanding.
- Sacrifice.

He once taught people to count the cost before building.

Discipleship isn't impulsive enthusiasm.

It's intentional allegiance.

As you step forward, ask not only:

"What career will I choose?"

But:

"What obedience will I embrace?"

Identity Before Performance

At Jesus' baptism, before any public ministry, the Father declared his pleasure.

Beloved before performance.

Graduates, the world will measure you by output.

- Titles.
- Income.
- Influence.

But heaven measures identity differently.
You are not loved because you achieve.
You achieve because you are loved.
Anchor your identity in Christ, not your résumé.

From Eyewitness to Witness

The disciples began as observers.
They became witnesses.
You may not see what they saw.
But you carry what they carried.

- Hope.
- Truth.
- Grace.
- Mission.

Graduation isn't simply advancement.
It's deployment.
The world doesn't need more credentials.
It needs more character.
It doesn't need more noise.
It needs more light.

What Commissioning Means

To commission means to send with purpose.

- Not drift.
- Not wander.
- Not chase applause.

But live intentionally.

- In your workplace, reflect integrity.
- In your friendships, reflect compassion.
- In your decisions, reflect wisdom.
- In your ambitions, reflect surrender.

A Question for All of Us

The call to follow Christ doesn't expire with age or stage of life.

Will we keep following or quietly settle in place?

- Have we settled into comfort?
  Or are we still following?
- Have we grown stationary?
  Or are we still sent?

The call remains the same:
"Follow me."

The Next Step

Graduates, today isn't the *finish* line.

It's the *starting* line.

- The One who called fishermen calls you.
- The One who empowered ordinary disciples empowers you.
- The One who reigns sends you.

So go.
Not merely to build a life.
But to build the Kingdom.
Follow him.

Commissioning Prayer

Lord Jesus,

You called ordinary people and changed the world through them.

Today, we commission these graduates.

- Guard their identity.
- Strengthen their courage.
- Guide their decisions.

And use their lives for your Kingdom.

Amen.

13. MEMORIAL SERVICE:
Death Is Not Final

Introduction: Grief Is Real

In moments of loss and sorrow, when hearts are heavy and hope feels buried, we are reminded that grief is a deeply human response to love.

- There are tears.
- Memories.
- Questions.

Grief isn't weakness.
It's love with nowhere to go.
When someone we love is gone, it feels like a door has closed forever.

The disciples once felt that way.

- They had walked with Jesus.
- Heard his voice.
- Watched his miracles.

And then:
"Jesus is nailed to the cross and dies."
Hope seemed buried.
A stone sealed the tomb.
And everything felt finished.

The Silence of Loss

There is something quiet about loss.

- After the service ends.
- After the flowers fade.
- After the visitors leave.

Silence.
The disciples experienced that silence.
Saturday.

- No miracles.
- No explanations.
- No visible hope.

Have you ever lived in a "Saturday"?

- Between promise and fulfillment.
- Between prayer and an answer.

Grief often feels like that.
But Scripture reminds us:
Silence doesn't mean absence.
God is still working when we cannot see him.

The Empty Tomb Changed Everything

Then came Sunday.
The tomb is opened, and people can't find Jesus' body.
The stone was not the end.
It was the doorway to something greater.
The resurrection doesn't erase grief.
But it transforms it.
Because if Christ conquered death, then death isn't final.
It isn't the ultimate authority.
It isn't the last word.

Jesus Understands Our Sorrow

God who brings life out of death is also the God who meets us tenderly in our deepest sorrow.

Before he raised Lazarus, Jesus wept.

He knew resurrection was coming.

And still, he wept.

That tells us something profound:

God doesn't dismiss grief.

He enters it.

When we stand beside a casket, we don't stand alone.

The One who conquered death also understands loss.

The Promise of Life

Resurrection stands at the heart of Christian hope, because it declares that death doesn't have the final word.

The resurrection isn't symbolic comfort.

It's historical victory.

Jesus did not simply teach about life.

He demonstrated power over the grave.

After his resurrection:

"Jesus appears to his disciples for the first time."

- Fear turned to courage.
- Despair turned to proclamation.

Because if the grave cannot hold him, it cannot ultimately hold those who belong to him.

For those who trust Christ, death isn't a wall.

It's a doorway.

Remembering with Hope

Today we remember.

We celebrate life.

Moments shared.

Character displayed.
Memory is sacred.
But memory isn't our only comfort.
Our comfort is promise.
Because the risen Christ reigns.
The disciples watched Jesus ascend into the clouds.
Ascension means he is alive now.
Reigning now.
Preparing now.
Our hope isn't in vague spirituality.
It's in a living King.

What This Means for Us

Grief reminds us of something important:

- Life is fragile.
- Time is limited.
- Love matters.
- And eternity is real.

A memorial service isn't only reflection.
It's invitation.
If Christ conquered death, then trusting him matters.
Because resurrection isn't automatic.
It's anchored in relationship with the risen Lord.

The Stone Is Not the End

On Friday, a stone sealed a tomb.

On Sunday, it was moved.

Today, as we stand in grief, it may feel like a stone rests on our hearts.

But resurrection promises:

- The stone isn't the end.
- The story isn't over.

- The separation isn't forever.

In Christ, hope outlives sorrow.

Holding Both Tears and Hope

Today we hold two things at once:

Tears.

And hope.

We don't deny sorrow.

But we don't surrender to despair.

Because the same Jesus who walked out of a tomb offers life beyond it.

And so we grieve.

But not as those without hope.

Closing Prayer

Lord Jesus,

You are the resurrection and the life.

Comfort every grieving heart here today.

Hold those who feel fragile.

Strengthen those who feel empty.

And remind us that the grave isn't the end for those who belong to you.

Amen.

14. DISCIPLESHIP SUNDAY: Follow Me

Introduction: Many Admire. Few Follow

It's possible to admire Jesus without following him.

- To quote him.
- To sing about him.
- To appreciate his teaching.

But admiration isn't discipleship.

At the beginning of his ministry, Jesus did not say:

- "Like me."
- "Agree with me."
- "Be inspired by me."

He said: "Follow me."

Discipleship is movement.

It's direction.

It's allegiance.

The Call Is Personal

In the narrative of *Eyewitness*, Jesus calls ordinary men—fishermen, tax collectors—and invites them into relationship before responsibility.

He doesn't begin with policy.

He begins with proximity.

"Follow me."

Not merely, "Learn about me."

"Walk with me."

Discipleship begins with presence.

- Before public ministry.
- Before miracles.
- Before crowds.

He calls people to himself.

The Kingdom Is Different

In his teaching, Jesus reshapes everything.

He speaks of:

- Loving enemies.
- Giving in secret.
- Forgiving endlessly.
- Seeking treasure in Heaven.

This isn't behavior modification.

It's heart transformation.

Discipleship isn't external compliance.

It's internal change.

You can attend church for years and never let the King reshape your heart.

But true discipleship touches:

- Motives.
- Speech.
- Ambition.
- Relationships.

Authority Demands Response

From the earliest days of his ministry, the central question was not merely what he taught but whether people would acknowledge his authority over their lives.

Religious leaders questioned Jesus' authority.

The issue was never simply theology.

It was lordship.
Who rules?
Discipleship is submission to authority.
Not partial.
Not seasonal.
Total.
We live in a culture that prizes autonomy.
Jesus calls for surrender.
You cannot *follow* and *lead* at the same time.

Count the Cost

Jesus did not hide the difficulty.

- He spoke about counting the cost before building.
- He warned that following him may divide families.
- He told stories of narrow gates and difficult roads.

Why?
Because discipleship isn't impulsive enthusiasm.
It's sustained obedience.
Grace is free.
Discipleship costs.

- Time.
- Comfort.
- Reputation.
- Self-rule.

But what you gain is far greater.

Fruit Is the Evidence

In his teaching, Jesus made something clear:
A tree is known by its fruit.
Discipleship isn't measured by attendance.
It's measured by transformation.

Are you growing in:

- Humility?
- Patience?
- Integrity?
- Compassion?

Not perfection.
But progress.
Formation is slow.
But it is visible.

From Believer to Witness

At one point:

Jesus sent another seventy-two disciples into the fields of ministry.

He multiplies disciples.

Discipleship is never meant to stop with us.

- We follow.
- We grow.
- We go.
- We help others follow.

A disciple who doesn't disciple is incomplete.
The Church doesn't exist to produce consumers.
It exists to form disciples who form disciples.

What Discipleship Looks Like Today

Discipleship looks like:

- Daily Scripture engagement.
- Intentional prayer.
- Honest accountability.
- Serving consistently.
- Giving generously.

- Sharing boldly.

It isn't dramatic.
It's faithful.
Day after day.
Decision after decision.

The Question

Every person who encounters Jesus must decide whether they will admire him from a distance, or truly follow him.

- Are you a fan?
  Or a follower?
- Are you informed?
  Or transformed?
- Have you added Jesus to your life?
  Or surrendered your life to him?

Discipleship isn't an elective.
It's the call.

Take the Next Step

Jesus still says:
"Follow Me."
Not someday.
Not when convenient.
Now.
Discipleship isn't about achieving greatness.
It's about reflecting Christ.
Take the next step.
Join a group.
Confess what needs confession.
Serve where needed.
Commit where hesitant.
Follow him.

Closing Prayer

Lord Jesus,

You did not call us to observe you.

You called us to follow you.

Expose where we are casual.

Strengthen where we are weak.

Form us into true disciples who reflect your character and multiply your mission.

Amen.

15. STEWARDSHIP SUNDAY: Faithful with What Is His

Introduction: It Was Never Yours

We speak of:

- "My money."
- "My time."
- "My abilities."
- "My resources."

But Scripture gently corrects that language.
Everything we have is entrusted.
Not owned.
Stewardship begins with this truth:
It was never ours to begin with.

The Widow Who Gave Everything

In the final week of his ministry:
A widow gave everything to God.
Many wealthy people gave large sums.

- Visible.
- Impressive.

But Jesus noticed the widow.
Not because of the amount.
Because of the surrender.
She did not give leftovers.
She gave livelihood.
Heaven measures differently.

Not volume.
But trust.

Stewardship Is a Heart Issue

Money reveals allegiance.

Where your treasure is, there your heart will be also.

The widow's gift was not financial strategy.

It was worship.

Stewardship isn't about percentages first.

It's about posture.

Do we trust God enough to release control?

The Parable of the Talents

Later, Jesus tells a story:

"People have a responsibility to use what they have been given."

A master entrusts resources to servants.

Different amounts.

Same expectation:

Faithfulness.

Two servants invest.

One buries.

The issue isn't comparison.

It's response.

The master doesn't demand equal results.

He commends faithful use.

What Was the Real Problem?

The servant who buried the talent was not wicked because he lost money.

He was paralyzed by fear.

He did not trust the master's character.

He hid what was entrusted.

Fear always buries what faith multiplies.
Stewardship requires courage.

- To invest.
- To risk.
- To trust.

Stewardship Is More than Money

Talents represent more than currency.
They represent:

- Time.
- Influence.
- Skills.
- Relationships.
- Opportunities

Some have more visible platforms.
Others have quieter spheres.
But all are entrusted.
And all will answer.

Eternal Accountability

Beyond how we manage what we have at the moment, stewardship considers the day when our lives will be reviewed before the King.

Not condemnation for believers.
But accountability.
One day we will stand before the King.
And the question will not be:
"How much did you accumulate?"
But:
"How faithful were you with what I gave?"

The Danger of Consumer Christianity

We live in a culture of consumption.

- Acquire.
- Upgrade.
- Accumulate.

But discipleship moves in the opposite direction.

- Give.
- Serve.
- Invest.

The Church isn't sustained by spectators.
It thrives through stewards.
Stewardship fuels mission.
It funds compassion.
It advances the Gospel.

The Greatest Gift

Ultimately, stewardship reflects the Gospel.

God gave first.

The Lamb was given.

"Look! The Lamb of God, who takes away the sin of the world."

We give because he gave.

Generosity flows from grace.

When we release resources, we reflect the heart of Christ.

The Question

Stewardship ultimately asks how we handle what God has placed in our care.

- Are we faithful?
  Or fearful?

- Are we investing?
  Or burying?
- Are we trusting God with everything?
  Or compartmentalizing?

Stewardship isn't about pressure.
It's about participation in God's work.

Well Done

Imagine hearing these words:
"Well done, good and faithful servant."
Not *wealthy* servant.
Not *impressive* servant.
Faithful servant.
The widow heard it in Heaven.
The investing servants heard it in the parable.
May we hear it in eternity.
Be faithful.
With what is his.

Closing Prayer

Lord Jesus,
Everything we have is from you.
Guard us from fear.
Free us from greed.
Teach us to trust you fully.
Make us faithful stewards of time, talent, and treasure.
Amen.

Study Group Sessons

Introductory Session: Why *Eyewitness*? Seeing the Whole Story

Purpose

By the end of this session participants will:

- Understand why the Gospels can feel fragmented.
- Appreciate the value of a chronological narrative.
- See Jesus as more than isolated stories.
- Commit to engaging the full journey.

Welcome and Opening (10 min.)

If someone asked you to tell the life story of Jesus in five minutes, where would you begin—and where would you end?

Let several people respond.

You'll likely hear:

- Bethlehem.
- Christmas.
- Sermon on the Mount.
- Miracles.
- The Cross.
- The Resurrection.

Then say:

Most of us know pieces. But can we see the flow?

The Problem We Don't Know We Have (10 min.)

Explain:

When we read Matthew, Mark, Luke, and John separately, we get:

- Repeated stories.
- Different details.
- Different sequences.
- Different emphases.

That's not a flaw. It's four eyewitnesses giving their perspective.

But imagine watching four documentaries about the same person, each arranged differently.

Now, read this idea aloud:

"Many people have read the Gospels but struggle to visualize the events in their complete, chronological form."

Ask:

- Why do you think chronology matters?
- Does order change understanding?

Guide them to see that chronology shows:

- Growth of opposition.
- Movement of ministry.
- Escalation toward the cross.
- Intentional timing.

Jesus' ministry was not random. It unfolded deliberately.

Reading Together: The Beginning (15 min.)

Have someone read aloud from the chapter: "Eyewitnesses begin their amazing testimony":

In the beginning, God created the heavens and the earth…

Then read:
The Word already existed… Life itself came from him…

Pause and ask:

- Why begin before Bethlehem?
- What changes when we see Jesus as Creator before Savior?
- How does this shape the rest of the story?

Key Insight:

- This story doesn't begin in a manger.
  It begins in eternity.
- The birth isn't the beginning.
  It's an arrival.

What This Study Will Do (10 min.)

Explain the twelve-week journey ahead.

We will walk through:

- Preparation.
- Public ministry.
- Growing conflict.
- Jerusalem.
- The cross.
- Resurrection.
- Ascension.

Say:

- This isn't a devotional hop-through. This is a narrative journey.

Encourage:

- Read assigned chapters weekly.
- Notice transitions.
- Watch emotional tone shift.
- Observe how miracles increase opposition.

Seeing Jesus as a Person, Not Just Events (15 min.)

Ask:

- What single scene of Jesus stands out most in your memory?
- What emotions do you associate with him?

Then discuss what many know:

- Baby Jesus.
- Miracle Jesus.
- Crucified Jesus.

But few trace:

- Rejected Jesus.
- Weary Jesus.
- Strategic Jesus.
- Confrontational Jesus.
- Grieved Jesus.

This study will help us see:

- Not just what Jesus did. But who he revealed himself to be.

Group Discussion Questions (20 min.)

- Why do you think God gave us four Gospel accounts instead of one?

- What happens when we read isolated stories instead of the full narrative?
- What do you hope to understand more clearly by the end of this study?
- If someone says, "I already know the story of Jesus," how would you respond?

Encourage honest reflection.

Personal Reflection Exercise (10 min.)

Hand out paper or ask participants to write in their journal:

- In just one sentence, write your answer to this question: Who is Jesus?
- Collect them or ask them to keep them sealed until the final session.

Tell them:

- At the end of twelve sessions, you'll write that sentence again.

Setting Expectations (5 min.)

Encourage people to get the most out of this study:

- Attend consistently.
- Read assigned chapters.
- Engage openly.
- Ask difficult questions.
- Listen respectfully.

Remind them:

- This isn't about accumulating information.
  It's about encountering Christ.

Closing Thought

Say slowly:

- When the disciples walked with Jesus, they didn't know how the story would end.
- We do.
- And yet—when we slow down and walk through it carefully, something changes.

We move from familiarity…

- To clarity.
- To conviction.
- To worship.

Closing Prayer

Pray:

- For open eyes.
- For softened hearts.
- For deeper understanding.
- For transformation.

Assignment for the Next Meeting

Read the chapters "Mary visits her aunt Elizabeth" to "Disciples of John the Baptizer meet Jesus for the first time":

- John the Baptizer.
- Jesus' baptism.
- Temptation.
- First followers.

Come ready to discuss:
Why does identity come before ministry?

STUDY 1:
Preparation and Identity

Chapters Covered: "Mary visits her aunt Elizabeth" to "Disciples of John the Baptizer meet Jesus for the first time" (Mary, John the Baptizer, Baptism, Temptation, First Followers).

Session Purpose

By the end of this session participants will:

- Understand why identity precedes ministry.
- Recognize the role of preparation in God's plan.
- See how Jesus' baptism and temptation reveal his mission.
- Reflect on their own identity in Christ.

Opening Question (10 min.)

Ask:

- When you introduce yourself to someone new, what do you say first?
- (Occupation? Family? Location? Interests?)

Then ask:

- If someone introduced Jesus before he performed a single miracle, what would that person say?

Transition:

- Before Jesus healed anyone, preached publicly, or called twelve apostles—heaven spoke.

John the Baptizer: Preparing the Way (15 min.)

Read aloud from the chapter: "John, son of Zechariah, becomes John the Baptizer":

"Repent," he said, "for the Kingdom of Heaven is near."

Ask:

- Why does preparation begin with repentance?
- Why didn't the Messiah simply arrive without warning?

Discuss:

- John's message was confrontation, not comfort.

He told religious leaders:

- *"You bunch of snakes. Who warned you to flee God's judgment?"*

Reflection:

- God rarely moves suddenly without preparing hearts first.

Ask:

- What does repentance actually mean?
- Why is repentance foundational to seeing Jesus clearly?

The Baptism of Jesus: Heaven Speaks (15 min.)

Read from the chapter "John baptizes Jesus":

As Jesus came up out of the water and prayed, the sky opened, and the Spirit of God descended like a dove, resting upon him. A voice spoke from above: "You are my son, whom I love. I am well pleased with you."

Ask:

- Why was baptism necessary if Jesus had no sin?
- What stands out in the Father's declaration?

Key Teaching Point:

- The Father's approval came *before* public ministry.

Jesus had not yet:

- Preached.
- Healed.
- Multiplied bread.
- Raised the dead.

Yet Heaven declared:
"I am well pleased with you."

Discuss:

- How does this challenge performance-based identity?
- What would change if we lived from approval instead of for approval?

The Temptation: Identity Tested (15 min.)

Read from the chapter "The Holy Spirit leads Jesus to an encounter with Satan":

"Since you are the Son of God, command these stones to become bread."

Notice Satan's strategy: *"Since you are…"*

- The temptation isn't merely about bread.
  It's about identity.

Continue reading:
"People do not live by bread only but by everything God says."

"You must not test the Lord your God."

"Love the Lord your God and serve him only, with all your heart and soul."

Ask: What categories of temptation do you see here?

- Physical need?
- Pride?
- Power?

Discuss:

- Every temptation was answered with Scripture.

Question:

- Why is Scripture essential in moments of testing?

The Lamb of God: Purpose Declared (10 min.)

Read from the chapter "John the Baptizer recognizes Jesus as the Lamb of God":

"Look! The Lamb of God, who takes away the sin of the world."

Ask:

- Why "Lamb"?
- What does that foreshadow?

Discuss:

- Before the cross ever happened publicly, the mission was declared clearly.
- Jesus did not discover his purpose later.
- He walked toward it from the beginning.

First Followers: Come and See (10 min.)

Read from the chapter "Disciples of John the Baptizer meet Jesus for the first time":

"Come and see."

Ask:

- Why doesn't Jesus argue or debate here?
- What does invitation teach us about evangelism?

Notice Nathanael's confession:

"Teacher! You really are the Son of God, the King of Israel."

Discussion:

- Recognition grows through encounter.

Group Discussion Questions (20 min.)

- Why do you think God prepared the way through John instead of sending Jesus suddenly?
- What does the Father's declaration at baptism mean for how we understand identity?
- How does Satan's temptation strategy still operate today?
- Why is Scripture the weapon Jesus used in every temptation?
- What does "Lamb of God" tell us about the direction this story is heading?

Encourage interaction.

Personal Application (10 min.)

Ask members to reflect silently:

- Where do I struggle with identity?
- Do I live *from* approval or *for* approval?

- What temptation most often challenges my identity in Christ?

Invite prayer in pairs or small clusters.

Closing Thought

Everything Jesus did flowed from who he was.

- Before the miracles…
- Before the crowds…
- Before the cross…

Jesus was declared the Son.
His identity anchored his obedience.
And his obedience fulfilled his mission.

Assignment for the Next Meeting

Read the chapters "The wedding feast continues after Jesus changes water into wine" to "Peter's mother-in-law is healed" (10 chapters).

Focus on:

- Water to wine.
- Temple cleansing.
- Nicodemus.
- Samaritan woman.

Come ready to discuss:

- Why does Jesus reveal himself privately before publicly?

STUDY 2:
First Signs & Private Conversations

Chapters Covered: "The wedding feast continues after Jesus changes water into wine" to "Peter's mother-in-law is healed" (Water to Wine, Temple Cleansing, Nicodemus, Samaritan Woman, Early Healings).

Session Purpose

By the end of this session participants will:

- See how Jesus reveals his identity progressively.
- Contrast private faith with public religion.
- Understand why miracles both attract and divide.
- Recognize that Jesus confronts systems before crowds.

Opening Question (10 min.)

Ask:

- When someone new enters your life, how do you decide whether to trust them?

Follow-up:

- Does trust grow more through public display or private conversation? Why?

Transition:

- In these chapters, Jesus performs his first miracle—but most of his identity is revealed in quiet conversations.

Water into Wine: A sign, Not a Show (15 min.)

Read from the chapter "The wedding feast continues after Jesus changes water into wine":

This miracle at Cana in Galilee was the first sign of Jesus' majesty, and his disciples believed in him.

Notice the word: *sign.*

Ask:

- What is a sign designed to do?
- Why was this miracle done quietly?

Discuss:

- Only servants and disciples knew what happened.
- It wasn't a spectacle.
- It wasn't a crowd performance.

Reflection on what Jesus' first miracle was about:

- Joy.
- Abundance.
- Quiet transformation.

Ask:

- What does saving "the best until now" reveal about God's nature?

Temple Cleansing: Holy Disruption (15 min.)

Read from the chapter "The merchants are driven out of the Temple":

"Do not make my Father's house a marketplace."

And:

"The scriptures say the Temple will be called a house of prayer for all nations, but you have turned it into a hangout for robbers."

Ask:

- Why does Jesus confront religious corruption so early?
- Why begin ministry with disruption?

Discuss:

- This isn't random anger.
  It's righteous alignment.

He is declaring:

- Authority.
- Ownership.
- Purity of worship.

Notice his bold statement:
"Destroy this temple and I will raise it up in three days."

Ask:

- Why speak in language people wouldn't understand?
- How often do we miss meaning because we hear literally what is spiritual?

Nicodemus: Religious but Searching (15 min.)

Read from the chapter "Nicodemus learns about spiritual birth":

"I can guarantee, you will never see the Kingdom of God unless you are born again."

Ask:

- Why does Jesus go straight to rebirth?
- What was Nicodemus missing?

Discuss Nicodemus:

- Educated.

- Respected.
- Religious.
- Sincere.

Yet Jesus says:

"No one can enter the Kingdom without being born of water and the Spirit."

Then read:

For God so loved the world that he gave his only son, so that everyone who believes in him will not die but will live forever.

Ask:

- Why is belief central?
- How is rebirth different from reform?

Reflection:

- Religion modifies behavior.
- Rebirth transforms nature.

The Samaritan Woman: An Unexpected Audience (15 min.)

Read from the chapter "A Samaritan woman comes for water and finds life":

"Everyone who drinks this water will thirst again. But those who drink the water I give will never become thirsty."

Ask:

- Why approach a Samaritan?
- Why reveal himself so directly here?

Then read:

"I am the Messiah."

Notice:

- To Nicodemus (a ruler), Jesus speaks in mystery.
- To a Samaritan woman (an outcast), he speaks plainly.

Ask:

- What does that teach us about spiritual hunger?
- Why does honesty open doors?

Discuss:

- She leaves her jar behind.

Symbolism:

- Old thirst abandoned.
- New purpose embraced.

Healing from a Distance: Faith Without Sight (10 min.)

Read from the chapter "A government official seeks healing for his sick son":

"You may go," Jesus said. "Your son will live."

And:

The man took Jesus at his word and left.

Ask:

- What kind of faith leaves before seeing?
- What does it mean to "take Jesus at his word"?

Discuss:

- The miracle happened before confirmation.
- Faith walked home trusting.

Nazareth Rejection: Familiarity Breeds Dismissal (10 min.)

Read from the chapter "At his boyhood home, Jesus is rejected":

"No prophet is accepted in his hometown."

Ask:

- Why does familiarity reduce reverence?
- How does proximity sometimes blind us?

Discuss:

- Those who watched him grow up couldn't see him clearly.

Ask:

- Can spiritual familiarity make us resistant? Why?

Group Discussion Questions (20 min.)

Why does Jesus begin with both celebration (Cana) and confrontation (Temple)?

- What difference do you see between Nicodemus and the Samaritan woman?
- What does "born again" mean, practically?
- Where do you struggle to take Jesus at his word without immediate proof?
- Why do some who know Jesus best reject him?

Encourage depth.

Personal Application (10 min.)

Ask participants to reflect:

- Am I more like Nicodemus or the Samaritan woman?

- Do I seek Jesus privately but hesitate publicly?
- Where might Jesus need to overturn tables in my life?

Invite prayer.

Closing Thought

In these chapters, Jesus:

- Brings joy.
- Disrupts corruption.
- Confronts religion.
- Offers rebirth.
- Breaks social barriers.
- Honors quiet faith.
- Faces rejection.

The Messiah isn't who people expected.
And that revelation begins in small rooms, not stadiums.

Assignment for the Next Meeting

Read the chapters "Jesus works after sunset" to "Jesus teaches about blessings that follow tough times."

Focus on:

- Expanding miracles.
- Calling Matthew.
- Sabbath confrontations.
- Selection of the Twelve.

Come ready to discuss:

- Why does authority increase opposition?

STUDY 3:
Authority & Opposition

Chapters Covered: "Jesus works after sunset" to "Jesus teaches about blessings that follow tough times" (Expanding Healings, Matthew Called, Sabbath Conflicts, Choosing the Twelve, Early Kingdom Teaching).

Session Purpose

By the end of this session participants will:

- Recognize how Jesus' authority grows publicly.
- Understand why miracles increase resistance.
- See how grace disrupts religious categories.
- Reflect on what it means to follow Jesus fully.

Opening Question (10 min.)

Ask:

- Have you ever seen someone challenge a system everyone else accepted?

Follow-up:

- What happens when authority confronts tradition?

Transition:

- As Jesus' ministry expands, so does the tension.

Expanding Healings: Power with Purpose (15 min.)

Read from the chapter "Jesus works after sunset."

After sunset, people brought to Jesus those who suffered from various diseases... When he touched them and spoke a few simple words, he healed each one.

Notice:

- No incantations.
- No spectacle.
- No struggle.

Authority is quiet, steady, and decisive.

Then read from the chapter "Fishermen are taught about fishing":

"You do not need to worry. From now on, you will fish for people."

Ask:

- Why move from healing bodies to calling disciples?
- What does "fishing for people" imply?

Discuss:

- Miracles draw crowds.
- Calling requires commitment.

The Leper: Compassion that Crosses Lines (10 min.)

Read from the chapter "A leper is cleansed":

"I want to." Moved with compassion, Jesus touched him. "Be cleansed."

Ask:

- Why touch a leper?
- What risk did that involve socially and ceremonially?

Discuss:

- The miracle was physical.
- The touch was relational.
- Authority isn't detached.

Forgiving Sin: The Real Controversy (15 min.)

Read from the chapter "A paralyzed man is lowered through the roof to see Jesus":

"Do not worry, my friend. Your sins are forgiven."

Religious leaders respond internally.

Then Jesus says:

"Which is easier to say, 'Your sins are forgiven,' or, 'Stand and walk'?"

Ask:

- Why is forgiving sin more controversial than healing paralysis?
- What is Jesus actually proving?

Discuss:

- Healing validates authority.
- Forgiveness reveals divinity.
- This moment escalates everything.

Calling Matthew: Grace that Offends (15 min.)

Read from the chapter "Matthew is invited to follow Jesus":

"Follow me," Jesus said. Matthew got up, left everything, and followed.

Then read:

"Healthy people do not need a doctor. The sick do."

And:

"I have not come to invite to repentance those who think they are righteous. I have come for those who know they are sinners."

Ask:

- Why does grace offend religious observers?
- Why eat with tax collectors?

Discuss who Matthew was:

- Collaborator.
- Exploiter.
- Socially rejected.

Yet Jesus:

- Calls him.
- Eats with him.
- Defends him.

Authority redefines worth.

Sabbath Confrontations: Lord of Rest (15 min.)

Read from the chapter "The disciples don't follow religious tradition":

"The Sabbath was made to meet the needs of the people, not people to meet the requirements of the Sabbath. The Son of Man is Lord even of the Sabbath."

Ask:

- What is Jesus claiming here?
- Why does this threaten religious leadership?

Then read from the chapter "A man with a shriveled hand is healed on the Sabbath":

"Is it lawful to do good or evil on the Sabbath, to save life or destroy it?"

Discuss how Jesus reframes:

- Law.
- Mercy.
- Intent.

Religion asks: "What is permitted?"
Jesus asks: "What is good?"

Choosing the Twelve: Strategic Intent (10 min.)

For the chapter "Jesus selects twelve apostles out of his group of followers":

Ask:

- Why twelve?
- Why these particular men?

Discuss who they were not:

- Scholars.
- Priests.
- Political leaders.

But they were:

- Fishermen.
- Tax collector.
- Zealot.

Authority chooses unlikely vessels.

Kingdom Values: Blessed Are… (10 min.)

From the chapter "Jesus teaches about blessings that follow tough times":

Ask:

- Why would the Kingdom bless hardship?

- How does this reverse cultural thinking?

Discuss:

- Authority redefines success.

Group Discussion Questions (20 min.)

- Why do miracles increase scrutiny?
- What stands out most about Jesus' authority?
- Why is forgiveness more threatening than healing?
- How does Jesus' treatment of Matthew challenge modern church culture?
- Where might we prioritize rule over mercy?
- What does it mean today that Jesus is "Lord of the Sabbath"?

Encourage depth and honesty.

Personal Application (10 min.)

Invite quiet reflection:

- Where do I resist Jesus' authority?
- Am I more comfortable with healing than forgiveness?
- Do I follow him casually or fully like Matthew?

Encourage prayer in small clusters.

Closing Thought

In these chapters:

- Authority grows.
- Crowds multiply.
- Opposition intensifies.

Jesus isn't merely compassionate.
He is sovereign.
And sovereignty disrupts systems.

Assignment for the Next Meeting

Read the chapters "God's people are to let their light shine" to "Jesus describes what the Kingdom of God is like."

Focus on:

- Sermon teachings.
- Prayer.
- Treasure.
- Kingdom parables.

Come ready to discuss:

- What kind of world does the Kingdom of God create?

STUDY 4:
Kingdom Principles

Chapters Covered: "God's people are to let their light shine" to "Jesus describes what the Kingdom of God is like" (Light, Righteousness, Enemies, Prayer, Treasure, Kingdom Parables).

Session Purpose

By the end of this session participants will:

- Understand how Jesus defines Kingdom righteousness.
- Recognize how the Kingdom reverses cultural values.
- Evaluate what they treasure most.
- See why Jesus teaches in parables.

Opening Question (10 min.)

Ask:

- If you could redesign society from the ground up, what values would you build it on?

Follow-up:

- How would that society differ from the one we live in now?

Transition:

- In these chapters, Jesus describes a Kingdom that doesn't operate like ours.

Let Your Light Shine (10 min.)

From the chapter "God's people are to let their light shine":

Ask:

- What does light do?
- Why is light never self-focused?

Discuss light:

- Reveals.
- Guides.
- Exposes.
- Warms.

Reflection:

- Kingdom citizens are not hidden believers.
  They are visible witnesses.

Ask:

- Where are you most tempted to dim your light?

Righteousness that Goes Deeper (15 min.)

From the chapter "God seeks righteous behavior that is more than the Law required":

Ask:

- What does it mean to go beyond external obedience?
- Why is inward righteousness harder?

Discuss:

- The Law said: Do not murder.
  Jesus teaches: Do not harbor hatred.

- The Law said: Do not commit adultery.
  Jesus teaches: Guard your heart.

Kingdom righteousness moves from behavior to motive.

Ask:

- Why does motive matter so much to God?

Loving Enemies: Radical Kingdom Ethic (15 min.)

From the chapter "People are to show kindness to even their enemies":

Ask:

- Why is loving enemies central to Kingdom life?
- What makes this command so disruptive?

Discuss how, in most systems:

- Loyalty is rewarded.
- Enemies are punished.

In God's Kingdom:

- Mercy extends beyond boundaries.

Ask:

- What enemy category is hardest for you to love?
- Is loving enemies passive or active?

Jesus Teaches About Prayer (15 min.)

From the chapter "Jesus teaches about prayer," discuss what Jesus emphasizes about prayer:

- Not performance.
- Not public display.
- Not empty repetition.

Prayer is relational alignment.

Ask:

- How is prayer different from religious speech?
- What does it mean to pray "Your Kingdom come"?

Reflection:

- Prayer trains the heart to desire what God desires.

Treasure and Priority (15 min.)

From the chapter "What you treasure needs to have lasting value":

Ask:

- What reveals what we truly treasure?
- How do we measure lasting value?

Discuss what Jesus teaches:

- Where your treasure is, your heart follows.
- Earthly wealth decays.
- Eternal investment endures.

Ask:

- If someone examined your calendar and spending, what would they conclude that you treasure?

Principles of God's Kingdom (10 min.)

From the chapter "Jesus teaches the principles of God's Kingdom":

Discuss themes:

- Ask, seek, knock.

- Treat others as you want to be treated.
- Enter through the narrow gate.

Ask:

- Why is the narrow gate narrow?
- What makes the wide road attractive?

Reflection:

- The Kingdom is open to all.
- But not everything fits through the gate.

Why Parables (10 min.)

From the chapters "Jesus uses a farming illustration to teach about hearing God's word" and "Jesus describes what the Kingdom of God is like":

Ask:

- Why teach through stories?
- What do parables require from listeners?

Discuss how parables:

- Invite reflection.
- Separate curiosity from commitment.
- Reveal truth to those willing to receive it.

Ask:

- What kind of soil are you right now?

Group Discussion Questions (20 min.)

- What Kingdom teaching challenges you most?
- Why does Jesus focus so heavily on the heart?
- What does loving enemies look like, practically?

- How does prayer reshape desire?
- What competes most for your treasure?
- What kind of soil best describes your spiritual condition?

Encourage transparency.

Personal Application (10 min.)

Invite silent reflection:

- Where is my righteousness mostly external?
- Who do I need to forgive or bless?
- What treasure needs re-evaluation?
- Is my faith reactive or rooted?

Encourage prayer in small groups.

Closing Thought

In these chapters, Jesus describes a Kingdom that:

- Values humility over status.
- Mercy over ritual.
- Motive over appearance.
- Treasure over accumulation.
- Depth over popularity.

This isn't reform.
This is reversal.
The Kingdom of God isn't built by power.
It's built by transformed hearts.

Assignment for the Next Meeting

Read the chapters "Jesus calms a violent storm" to "With five loaves, Jesus feeds five thousand men."

Focus on:

- Calming the storm.
- Delivering the possessed.
- Raising Jairus's daughter.
- Feeding five thousand.

Come ready to discuss:

- What does Jesus have authority over?

STUDY 5:
Power Over Nature & Death

Chapters Covered: "Jesus calms a violent storm" to "With five loaves, Jesus feeds five thousand men" (Calming the Storm, Legion Delivered, Jairus's Daughter, Feeding 5,000).

Session Purpose

By the end of this session participants will:

- Recognize the scope of Jesus' authority.
- Understand the difference between fear and faith.
- See how miracles reveal identity.
- Reflect on what storms test in their own lives.

Opening Question (10 min.)

Ask:

- What situation in life has made you feel most out-of-control?

Follow-up:

- When you cannot control circumstances, what do you rely on?

Transition:

- In these chapters, the disciples discover something unsettling.

- Jesus isn't only a teacher.
  He commands storms.

Calming the Storm: Authority Over Creation (15 min.)

Read from the chapter "Jesus calms a violent storm." Then ask someone to summarize the scene:

- Boat.
- Wind.
- Panic.
- Jesus asleep.

Ask:

- Why would Jesus sleep through the storm?
- What does that reveal?

Discuss what the disciples ask:

- "Who is this?"
- That question is central.

Reflection on what they had seen:

- Healings.
- Teachings.
- Authority over disease.

But wind and waves?
That belongs to God alone.

Ask:

- What storms test your trust most?

Legion: Authority Over Demons (15 min.)

From the chapter "Jesus delivers a man who was possessed by many evil spirits":

Discuss:

- The man isolated.
- Bound.
- Feared.
- Tormented.

Ask:

- Why does Jesus cross the sea for one man?
- What does that say about value?

Discuss:

- Authority isn't selective.
  It confronts darkness directly.

Reflection:

- After deliverance, the healed man wants to follow.
- But Jesus sends him back to tell his story.

Ask:

- Why send him home instead of letting him travel with the Twelve?

Jairus and The Interrupted Miracle (15 min.)

From the chapter "Jairus's daughter is raised from the dead":

Discuss the tension:

- A desperate father.
- A dying child.

- An interruption (the woman with the issue of blood).
- Delay.

Ask:

- Why does Jesus allow delay?
- What happens to faith during waiting?

Then reflect:

- Death seems final.
- But for Jesus, it isn't ultimate.

Ask:

- What situations feel "too late" in your life?

Feeding Five Thousand: Authority Over Scarcity (15 min.)

From the chapter "With five loaves, Jesus feeds five thousand men":

Discuss:

- Insufficient resources.
- Overwhelming need.
- Disciples calculating limits.

Ask:

- Why involve the disciples in distribution?
- Why multiply through their hands?

Reflection:

- Scarcity is often the setting for revelation.

Ask:

- Where do you see only "five loaves" in your life?

The Growing Question (10 min.)

Across these chapters, authority expands:

- Wind obeys.
- Demons obey.
- Disease obeys.
- Death obeys.
- Bread multiplies.

Ask:

- What category remains outside his authority?
  Answer: Nothing.

Discuss:

- The question is no longer: Can he?
- The question becomes: Will we trust him?

Group Discussion Questions (20 min.)

- Which miracle stretches your faith most?
- Why do the disciples still fear after witnessing so much?
- What does the storm reveal about human panic?
- Why does Jesus prioritize the isolated demoniac?
- What role does waiting play in Jairus' story?
- How does scarcity reveal our assumptions about God?

Encourage depth.

Personal Application (10 min.)

Invite reflection:

- What storm am I facing?

- What fear dominates my thinking?
- Where do I see scarcity instead of sufficiency?
- Do I treat Jesus as Savior but not Sovereign?

Pray in small groups.

Closing Thought

In these chapters, Jesus demonstrates:

- He isn't merely compassionate.
- He isn't merely wise.
- He isn't merely prophetic.
- He is sovereign.
- Nature obeys him.
- Demons flee him.
- Death yields to him.
- Scarcity dissolves before him.

The only remaining question is:

- How well do we yield to his control?

Assignment for the Next Meeting

Read the chapters "Jesus walks with Peter on the water" to "Jesus teaches in the Temple."

Focus on:

- Bread of Life teaching.
- Traditions vs truth.
- Peter's confession.
- Transfiguration.
- Rising opposition.

Come ready to discuss:

- Why does clarity increase division?

STUDY 6:
Growing Opposition & Clear Identity

Chapters Covered: "Jesus walks with Peter on the water" to "Jesus teaches in the Temple" (Walking on Water, Bread of Life, Traditions Challenged, Peter's Confession, Transfiguration, Rising Tension in Jerusalem).

Session Purpose

By the end of this session participants will:

- Understand why revelation increases division.
- See how misunderstanding leads to departure.
- Recognize the turning point in Peter's confession.
- Reflect on what it means to follow a suffering Messiah.

Opening Question (10 min.)

Ask:

- Have you ever believed something strongly that others rejected? What did you do?

Follow-up:

- What happens when truth clarifies instead of softens?

Transition:

- In these chapters, Jesus becomes clearer.
- And as he becomes clearer, the crowd becomes smaller.

Walking on Water: Fear and Focus (10 min.)

From the chapter "Jesus walks with Peter on the water":

Ask:

- Why does Peter step out?
- Why does he sink?

Discuss:

- Faith steps.
- Fear sinks.

Reflection:

- Storms reveal focus.

Ask:

- What pulls your eyes away from Christ most quickly?

The Bread of Life: Hard Teaching (15 min.)

From the chapter "Jesus is the bread of life":

Discuss the setting:

- After feeding five thousand.
- After miraculous provision.
- Crowds seeking more bread.

But Jesus shifts from physical to spiritual hunger.

Ask:

- Why does the crowd resist when teaching becomes difficult?
- What is the difference between wanting provision and wanting transformation?

Reflection:

- Miracles attract.
- Teaching filters.

Traditions of Men: Heart Versus Habit (15 min.)

From the chapter "Traditions of men don't make people right with God":

Ask:

- Why are traditions so powerful?
- How can good traditions become barriers?

Discuss how Jesus exposes:

- External compliance.
- Internal distance.

Ask:

- What traditions might we confuse with spiritual life?

Reflection:

- Religion can preserve form while losing heart.

Peter's Confession: The Turning Point (15 min.)

From the chapter "Peter recognizes Jesus as the Messiah sent from God":

Ask:

- Why is this moment pivotal?
- Why does Jesus ask, "Who do you say I am?"

Discuss what crowds say:

- Prophet.

- Teacher.
- Miracle worker.

Peter says: Messiah.
Identity clarified.
But immediately after, Jesus predicts suffering.

Ask:

- Why does Peter struggle with a suffering Messiah?

Reflection:

- We often want a conquering Christ.
- But the cross is central.

The Transfiguration: Glory Veiled and Revealed (10 min.)

From the chapter "Three disciples see Jesus talk with Moses and Elijah":

Discuss:

- Law (Moses).
- Prophets (Elijah).
- Fulfillment (Jesus).

Ask:

- Why show glory briefly?
- Why return to normal life afterward?

Reflection:

- Revelation strengthens faith for coming difficulty.

Escalating Tension in Jerusalem (15 min.)

From the chapter "Jesus goes to Jerusalem unannounced,"

"Guards are sent to arrest Jesus," and "Jesus teaches in the Temple":

Ask:

- Why does opposition intensify?
- What threatens religious leaders most?

Discuss:

- It isn't miracles.
- It's authority.
- It's exposure.
- It's claim.

Clarity forces decision.

The Great Divide (10 min.)

Across these chapters:

- Some believe more deeply.
- Some walk away.
- Some plot murder.

Ask:

- Why does clarity not create unity?

Discuss:

- Truth divides when hearts resist.

Ask:

- Where might I resist truth because it disrupts comfort?

Group Discussion Questions (20 min.)

- Why do crowds thin when teaching becomes difficult?
- What traditions might blind us to spiritual reality?
- Why is Peter's confession both courageous and incomplete?
- What does it mean to follow a Messiah who suffers?
- Why does revelation create opposition instead of consensus?

Encourage honest dialogue.

Personal Application (10 min.)

Invite reflection:

- Do I follow Jesus for bread or for truth? Why?
- What part of his identity do I resist?
- Do I embrace both his glory and his cross?

Pray together.

Closing Thought

In these chapters:

Miracles continue.
But misunderstanding increases.
The crowd shifts from curiosity…

- To confusion.
- To conflict.

Jesus doesn't soften the message.
He sharpens it.
And every sharpened truth draws a line.

Assignment for the Next Meeting

Read the chapters "Jesus sends another seventy-two disciples into the fields of ministry" to "A builder must count the cost."

Focus on:

- The Good Samaritan.
- Warnings about hypocrisy.
- Counting the cost.
- Kingdom effort.

Come ready to discuss:

- What does following Jesus really cost?

This session centers on the cost, urgency, and seriousness of discipleship.

STUDY 7:
The Cost of Discipleship

Chapters Covered: "Jesus sends another seventy-two disciples into the fields of ministry" to "A builder must count the cost" (Sending the Seventy-Two, Good Samaritan, Hypocrisy Warnings, Greed, Readiness, Bearing Fruit, Counting the Cost)

Session Purpose

By the end of this session participants will:

- Understand that following Jesus involves sacrifice.
- Recognize how hypocrisy undermines discipleship.
- See how love defines true obedience.
- Reflect honestly on the cost they are willing to pay.

Opening Question (10 min.)

Ask:

- What is something valuable you acquired at one time that cost more than you expected?

Follow-up:

- When do we decide something is worth the cost?

Transition:

- In these chapters, Jesus makes something unmistakably clear: Following him is not casual.

Sent into the Fields: Participation, Not Observation (10 min.)

From the chapter "Jesus sends another seventy-two disciples into the fields of ministry":

Ask:

- Why send seventy-two?
- Why multiply messengers?

Discuss:

- Discipleship isn't spectator sport.
  It's a participatory mission.

Ask:

- Where has God sent you?
- Do you see your everyday life as mission field?

The Good Samaritan: Love that Crosses Lines (15 min.)

From the chapter "A good Samaritan helping a Jew shows how to love others":

Ask:

- Why choose a Samaritan as the hero?
- Who would be today's equivalent?

Discuss:

- Religious leaders passed by.
- An outsider stopped.
- The question shifts from: "Who is my neighbor?"
  to: "Will I be one?"

Ask:

- What prejudice must disciples overcome?

Warning Against Hypocrisy (15 min.)

From the chapter "Jesus warns against religious hypocrisy":

Discuss:

- Hypocrisy isn't weakness.
  It's pretense.

Ask:

- Why is hypocrisy so destructive?
- How can outward religion mask inward distance?

Reflection:

- The most dangerous spiritual condition is believing we are fine when we are not.

Ask:

- Where might image matter more than authenticity in your life?

Greed and False Security (10 min.)

From the chapter "A rich man shows how greed is never satisfied":

Ask:

- Why does wealth create spiritual risk?
- What illusion does greed offer?

Discuss what greed promises:

- Security.
- Control.

- Status.

But greed delivers:

- Anxiety.
- Isolation.
- Emptiness.

Reflection:

- What we cling to reveals what we trust.

Readiness and Fruitfulness (15 min.)

From the chapter "The Lord's coming requires constant readiness" and "Jesus stresses the importance of bearing fruit":

Ask:

- What does readiness look like, practically?
- What kind of fruit is Jesus describing?

Discuss:

- Readiness isn't panic.
  It's faithful consistency.
- Fruit isn't busyness.
  It's transformation.

Count the Cost (15 min.)

From the chapter "A builder must count the cost":

Ask:

- Why does Jesus use a construction analogy?
- What happens if you begin but cannot finish?

Discuss the fact that Jesus isn't hiding difficulty. He is clarifying it.

Discipleship requires:

- Priority shift.
- Loyalty shift.
- Identity shift.

Ask:

- What might following Jesus cost in today's culture?

Reflection:

- Grace is free.
- Discipleship is costly.

Group Discussion Questions (20 min.)

- Why does Jesus repeatedly stress seriousness?
- What is the greatest obstacle to loving like the Samaritan?
- Where does hypocrisy most easily creep in?
- What do you most fear losing if you fully follow Christ?
- What does counting the cost look like practically?
- Is readiness something you think about regularly?
- Encourage honesty.

Personal Application (10 min.)

Invite reflection:

- What cost am I avoiding?
- Is my discipleship convenient or committed?
- What fruit is visible in my life?

Pray together.

Closing Thought

In these chapters, Jesus makes no attempt to lower the bar. He raises it.

Discipleship is not:

- Occasional attendance.
- Verbal agreement.
- Cultural affiliation,

It's surrendered allegiance.
And surrender always costs something.
The question isn't whether it costs.
The question is whether he is worth it.

Assignment for the Next Meeting

Read the chapters "That which is lost is especially important" to "Zacchaeus climbs a tree to see Jesus."

Focus on:

- Lost sheep, coin, and son.
- Lazarus and the rich man.
- Zacchaeus.
- Faithfulness.

Come ready to discuss:

- What does Heaven celebrate?

STUDY 8
Lost and Found

Chapters Covered: "That which is lost is especially important" to "Zacchaeus climbs a tree to see Jesus" (The Lost Sheep, Coin, and Son; The Rich Man & Lazarus; Faithfulness; Zacchaeus; Eternal Perspective).

Session Purpose

By the end of this session participants will:

- Understand God's heart for the lost.
- Recognize the seriousness of eternal choices.
- Reflect on stewardship and faithfulness.
- See how true repentance produces visible change.

Opening Question (10 min.)

Ask:

- Have you ever lost something valuable and searched everywhere for it?

Follow-up:

- How did you feel when you found it?

Transition:

- In these chapters, Jesus tells us what God searches for—and what Heaven celebrates.

That Which Is Lost Is Important (15 min.)

From the chapter "That which is lost is especially important":

Discuss the three parables:

- Lost sheep.
- Lost coin.
- Lost son.

Ask:

- Why tell three versions of the same theme?
- What escalates in value each time?

Discuss:

- 1 sheep out of 100.
- 1 coin out of 10.
- 1 son out of 2.

The focus shifts from *possession* to *relationship*.

Ask:

- Which character do you most relate to—the wandering son or the resentful brother?

Reflection:

- Heaven doesn't celebrate perfection.
  It celebrates repentance.

The Older Brother: Religious Distance (10 min.)

Although obedient outwardly, the older brother's heart is cold.

Ask:

- Why is resentment spiritually dangerous?
- Can long-term obedience create entitlement?

Discuss:

- Lostness isn't only rebellion.
- It can be self-righteousness.

The Rich Man and Lazarus: Eternal Consequence (15 min.)

From the chapter "A dead man wants to tell his brothers about his eternal torment":

Ask:

- Why does Jesus tell such a sobering story?
- What does this reveal about eternity?

Discuss:

- Wealth doesn't equal favor.
- Poverty doesn't equal rejection.
- Death doesn't end awareness.

Ask:

- What does this parable challenge in modern thinking?

Reflection:

- Temporary comfort doesn't secure eternal destiny.

Faithfulness in Small Things (10 min.)

From the chapter "Jesus teaches on faithfulness" and "Servants must be faithful to their duties":

"Jesus teaches on faithfulness."

Ask:

- Why emphasize small responsibilities?
- How does daily faithfulness shape eternity?

Discuss:

- Faithfulness is quiet obedience.
- Heaven measures different from culture.

Zacchaeus: Visible Repentance (15 min.)

From the chapter "Zacchaeus climbs a tree to see Jesus":

Ask:

- Why climb a tree?
- What does desperation reveal?

Discuss Zacchaeus:

- Wealthy.
- Powerful.
- Socially rejected.
- Yet spiritually hungry.

After encountering Jesus, his response is restitution.

Ask:

- What does genuine repentance look like?
- Why is restitution important?

Reflection:

- Salvation is internal.
- Transformation becomes visible.

Stewardship and Eternal Rewards (10 min.)

From the chapter "People should recognize the value of eternal rewards":

Ask:

- What motivates long-term obedience?

- Do we think in eternal terms or immediate terms?

Discuss:

- The Kingdom perspective stretches beyond today.

The Central Question (5 min.)

Across these chapters:

- Heaven searches.
- Heaven rejoices.
- Eternity matters.
- Faithfulness counts.
- Repentance transforms.

Ask:

- What does Heaven celebrate?

Not:

- Wealth.
- Status.
- Appearance.

But:

- Repentance.
- Faithfulness.
- Humility.
- Return.

Group Discussion Questions (20 min.)

- Which lost parable speaks most to you?
- Why is the older brother harder to recognize in ourselves?
- What does the rich man's story reveal about urgency?
- Where are you being called to greater faithfulness?

- What visible evidence follows true repentance?
- How often do you think in eternal terms?
- Encourage transparency.

Personal Application (10 min.)

Invite quiet reflection:

- Am I spiritually drifting?
- Am I resentful of grace shown to others?
- Where do I need to make restitution?
- What eternal reward am I truly pursuing?

Pray in small groups.

Closing Thought

In these chapters, Jesus reveals:

- God searches.
- Heaven celebrates.
- Eternity waits.
- Faithfulness matters.

Lostness isn't the end.

Returning is.

And Heaven throws a party when even one person comes home.

Assignment for the Next Meeting

Read the chapters "Two blind men want to see" to "Jesus answers a question about the Messiah."

Focus on:

- Triumphant entry.
- Authority questioned.
- Greatest commandment.

- Rising confrontation.

Come ready to discuss:

- Why does praise so quickly turn to rejection?

STUDY 9:
The King Enters Jerusalem

Chapters Covered: "Two blind men want to see" to "Jesus answers a question about the Messiah" (Triumphant Entry, Authority Challenged, Parables of Judgment, Taxes, Resurrection Question, Greatest Commandment)

Session Purpose

By the end of this session participants will:

- Understand the significance of the Triumphant Entry.
- Recognize why religious leaders feel threatened.
- See how Jesus exposes shallow allegiance.
- Grasp the central commandment that anchors everything.

Opening Question (10 min.)

Ask:

- Have you ever seen public opinion change quickly?

Follow-up:

- Why does admiration sometimes turn into opposition?

Transition:

- In these chapters, Jesus receives public praise—and within days, leaders plan his death.

The Triumphant Entry: A Different Kind of King (15 min.)

From the chapter "People cheer as Jesus rides into Jerusalem on a donkey":

Ask:

- Why a donkey instead of a warhorse?
- What expectations did the crowd have?

Discuss what the crowd likely anticipated:

- Political overthrow.
- Roman defeat.
- National restoration.

But Jesus enters humbly.

Reflection:

- The crowd celebrates the Messiah they want.
- Not necessarily the Messiah he is.

Ask:

- Do we ever project our expectations onto Jesus? Why?

Authority Questioned (15 min.)

From the chapter "Religious leaders question Jesus' authority":

Ask:

- Why challenge his authority now?
- What threatens them most?

Discuss:

- Jesus teaches boldly.
- He exposes hypocrisy.

- He claims divine authority.

Authority threatens control.

Reflection:

- The issue isn't whether Jesus performs miracles. It's whether he rules.

Ask:

- Where might we resist Jesus' authority in subtle ways?

Parables of Judgment: Warning Signs (15 min.)

From the chapter "Sharecroppers kill the landowner's son" and "Jesus compares the Kingdom to a wedding feast":

Ask:

- Who do the sharecroppers represent?
- Why tell a wedding feast parable at this moment?

Discuss themes:

- Rejected messengers.
- Rejected Son.
- Consequences of refusal.
- Invitation extended beyond expected guests.

Reflection:

- The invitation is wide.
- Acceptance isn't automatic.

Ask:

- What does it mean to reject the invitation today?

Traps and Tests (15 min.)

From the chapter "Religious leaders seek to trap Jesus with a question about taxes" and "Jesus teaches about life after death":

Ask:

- Why try to trap Jesus politically?
- Why question resurrection?

Discuss the leaders' attempt:

- Political trap (taxes).
- Theological trap (resurrection).
- Legal trap (commandments).

Jesus answers with clarity and composure.

Reflection:

- Truth stands firm under scrutiny.

The Greatest Commandment: The Core (15 min.)

From the chapter "A man asks what the most important commandment is":

Discuss Jesus' answer:

- Love God fully.
- Love your neighbor.

Ask:

- Why reduce everything to love?
- What does loving God with all heart, soul, and mind mean?

Reflection:

- Religion multiplies rules.
- Jesus distills priority.
- Love isn't sentiment.
- It's allegiance.

Messiah Question: Revealing Identity (10 min.)

From the chapter "Jesus answers a question about the Messiah":

Ask:

- Why ask them whose son the Messiah is?
- What claim is Jesus making?

Discuss:

- He isn't merely David's descendant.
- He is David's Lord.
- The identity question becomes unavoidable.

The Shift (5 min.)

In these chapters:

- Crowds cheer.
- Leaders question.
- Parables warn.
- Traps fail.
- Truth clarifies.

The line is drawn.

Ask:

- Why does praise turn into plotting?

Discuss:

- Because Jesus refuses to become what they want him to be.

Group Discussion Questions (20 min.)

- What expectations did the crowd place on Jesus?
- Why is authority the central issue?
- What do the parables of judgment reveal about responsibility?
- Why does love summarize the Law?
- Where might we praise Jesus publicly but resist him privately?

Encourage thoughtful interaction.

Personal Application (10 min.)

Invite reflection:

- Do I want Jesus as Savior but not King?
- What expectations have I projected onto him?
- Is love truly the organizing principle of my life?

Pray together.

Closing Thought

In Jerusalem, everything accelerates.

- The King arrives.
- The leaders resist.
- The crowd wavers.
- The invitation stands.
- The cross approaches.

The question is no longer: Can he perform miracles?
The question is: Will we crown him?

Assignment for the Next Meeting

Read the chapters "Jesus condemns the religious leaders" to "Jesus compares God's judgment to the separation of sheep and goats."

Focus on:

- Condemnation of hypocrisy.
- End-time teaching.
- Ten virgins.
- Talents.
- Sheep and goats.

Come ready to discuss:

- What does readiness look like?

STUDY 10: Ready or Not

Chapters Covered: "Jesus condemns the religious leaders" to "Jesus compares God's judgment to the separation of sheep and goats" (Condemning Religious Leaders, Widow's Offering, End-Time Teaching, Ten Virgins, Talents, Sheep and Goats).

Session Purpose

By the end of this session participants will:

- Understand why Jesus speaks so strongly about hypocrisy.
- Recognize the urgency of readiness.
- Reflect on stewardship and accountability.
- Grasp the seriousness of eternal separation.

Opening Question (10 min.)

Ask:

- Have you ever been unprepared for something important?

Follow-up:

- What does preparation reveal about priority?

Transition:

- As Jesus' earthly ministry draws to a close, his tone sharpens.

The message becomes urgent.

Condemning Religious Hypocrisy (15 min.)

From the chapter "Jesus condemns the religious leaders":

Ask:

- Why such strong language?
- Why confront leaders publicly?

Discuss how the religious leaders:

- Knew Scripture.
- Held influence.
- Lacked humility.

Hypocrisy misleads others.

Reflection:

- The issue isn't imperfection.
  It's pretending.

Ask:

- Where might appearance overshadow authenticity in our lives?

The Widow's Offering: True Value (10 min.)

From the chapter "A widow gives everything to God":

Ask:

- Why highlight a small gift?
- What does "everything" mean here?

Discuss what Heaven measures:

- Sacrifice.
- Trust.
- Proportion.

Not:

- Visibility.
- Amount.
- Applause.

Reflection:

- God sees what others overlook.

Signs and Endurance (15 min.)

From the chapter "Jesus reveals what will happen before his return":

Ask:

- Why speak about future turmoil?
- Does this produce fear or faith? Why?

Discuss themes included:

- Deception.
- Conflict.
- Perseverance.

Reflection:

- Readiness isn't date-setting.
  It's faithfulness during uncertainty.

Ten Virgins: Watchfulness (15 min.)

From the chapter "A story about ten virgins shows the importance of being ready":

Ask:

- What distinguishes the wise from the foolish?
- Why can't readiness be borrowed?

Discuss:

- All were invited.
- All were waiting.
- Only some were prepared.

Reflection:

- Spiritual readiness is personal responsibility.

Ask:

- What does oil represent in your life?

Talents: Stewardship and Accountability (15 min.)

From the chapter "People have a responsibility to use what they have been given":

Ask:

- Why reward risk and confront fear?
- What does burying a talent reveal?

Discuss what stewardship involves:

- Trust.
- Initiative.
- Faithfulness.

Fear paralyzes.

Faith multiplies.

Reflection:

- What have you buried?

Sheep and Goats: Final Separation (15 min.)

From the chapter "Jesus compares God's judgment to the separation of sheep and goats":

Ask:

- What determines separation?
- Why focus on acts of mercy?

Discuss:

- The righteous are surprised.
- The condemned are surprised.
- Service to "the least" equals service to the King.

Reflection:

- Faith expresses itself through compassion.

The Thread that Connects These Chapters (5 min.)

Across these chapters:

- Hypocrisy is exposed.
- Sacrifice is honored.
- Future is revealed.
- Preparation is demanded.
- Stewardship is evaluated.
- Judgment is real.

Ask:

- What does readiness look like?

Discuss:

- Not anxiety.

But:

- Integrity.
- Generosity.
- Watchfulness.
- Faithfulness.
- Compassion.

Group Discussion Questions (20 min.)

- Why does Jesus confront hypocrisy so strongly?
- What does the widow teach us about trust?
- How should we respond to teachings about the end times?
- What talents might you be underusing?
- How does compassion reveal authentic faith?
- If Jesus returned today, what would you want him to find you doing?

Encourage thoughtful engagement.

Personal Application (10 min.)

Invite reflection:

- Am I spiritually prepared?
- Is there hidden hypocrisy I need to address?
- What gift am I called to multiply?
- Who are "the least" in my life?

Pray together.

Closing Thought

As the cross approaches, Jesus doesn't soften his message. He clarifies it.

- The Kingdom is coming.
- Readiness matters.
- Faithfulness counts.
- Compassion reveals allegiance.
- The door will close.
- The King will return.

The question is not if.
The question is whether we are ready.

Assignment for the Next Meeting

Read the chapters "Judas agrees to betray Jesus" to "Jesus is nailed to the cross and dies."

Focus on:

- Betrayal
- Last Supper
- Gethsemane
- Trial
- Crucifixion

Come ready to discuss:

- Why was the cross necessary?

STUDY 11:
The Passion

Chapters Covered: "Judas agrees to betray Jesus" to "Jesus is nailed to the cross and dies" (Betrayal, Last Supper, Gethsemane, Arrest, Trials, Crucifixion, Death).

Session Purpose

By the end of this session participants will:

- Understand the intentionality of the cross.
- Recognize the depth of Christ's obedience.
- Reflect on betrayal, fear, and surrender.
- Grasp what was accomplished through his death.

Opening Question (10 min.)

Ask:

- Have you ever experienced betrayal?

Follow-up:

- What hurts more—the act itself, or who committed it?

Transition:

- The final hours of Jesus' earthly ministry are marked by betrayal, abandonment, injustice—and deliberate obedience.

Judas: Betrayal from Within (10 min.)

From the chapter "Judas agrees to betray Jesus":

Ask:

- Why would one of the Twelve betray him?
- What warning does Judas represent?

Discuss:

- Betrayal doesn't come from distance.
  It comes from proximity without surrender.

Reflection:

- It's possible to walk near Jesus without yielding to him.

The Last Supper: A New Covenant (15 min.)

From the chapter "Jesus celebrates Passover with the disciples":

Discuss:

- Passover recalled deliverance from Egypt.
- Now, Jesus reframes it around himself.

Ask:

- Why connect his death to Passover?
- What does substitution mean?

Reflection:

- The Lamb of God, first identified early in the story, now prepares to fulfill that title.

Gethsemane: Surrender Under Pressure (15 min.)

From the chapter "Jesus prays at Gethsemane":

Ask:

- Why pray in anguish?
- What does this reveal about his humanity?

Discuss:

- Jesus wrestles with the cup.
- Yet he submits.
- Surrender isn't an absence of struggle.
- It's obedience, despite the struggle.

Ask:

- What does surrender look like in your life?

The Trials: Injustice Exposed (15 min.)

From the chapter "Jesus is tried before Caiaphas" and "Jesus stands before Pilate":

Discuss:

- False accusations.
- Political pressure.
- Mob influence.

Ask:

- Why does Jesus remain largely silent?
- What kind of power is restraint?

Reflection:

- Authority isn't diminished by silence.
- It's displayed in control.

Crucifixion: Purpose, Not Tragedy (20 min.)

From the chapter "Jesus is nailed to the cross and dies":

- Pause before discussing.
- Allow a moment of silence.

Ask:

- Why was crucifixion chosen?
- What was accomplished at the cross?

Discuss the cross:

- Exposes sin.
- Absorbs judgment.
- Demonstrates love.
- Defeats death.

Earlier in the story, John the Baptizer declared:
"Look! The Lamb of God, who takes away the sin of the world."
Now, that declaration reaches fulfillment.

Reflection:

- This was not a plan gone wrong.
  It was the plan unfolding.

Abandonment and Loyalty (10 min.)

Discuss:

- Peter denies.
- Disciples scatter.
- Women remain.
- Joseph of Arimathea steps forward.

Ask:

- Why does fear silence some and embolden others?

- Where would you have stood?

Reflection:

- The cross reveals hearts.

Group Discussion Questions (20 min.)

- What part of the Passion narrative affects you most deeply?
- Why is surrender central in Gethsemane?
- How does silence function as strength?
- Why is the cross necessary rather than optional?
- What does the cross reveal about God's character?
- How does this story reshape your understanding of love?

Encourage reverence and depth.

Personal Application (10 min.)

Invite reflection:

- What have I not surrendered?
- Do I minimize the cost of the cross?
- How should the cross shape my daily living?

Pray together.

Closing Thought

In these chapters:

- Friends fail.
- Leaders manipulate.
- Crowds rage.
- Soldiers mock.
- The sky darkens.

And Jesus obeys.

- The cross isn't weakness.
- It's victory concealed in suffering.
- The Lamb was not overpowered.

He was offered.

Assignment for the Next Meeting

Read the chapters "Joseph of Arimathea and Nicodemus give Jesus a hasty burial before sundown" to "The disciples watch Jesus ascend into the clouds."

Focus on:

- Burial.
- Empty tomb.
- Appearances.
- Ascension.

Come ready to discuss:

- What changes because he lives?

STUDY 12 — Resurrection & Commission

Chapters Covered: "Joseph of Arimathea and Nicodemus give Jesus a hasty burial before sundown" to "The disciples watch Jesus ascend into the clouds" (Burial, Empty Tomb, Emmaus Road, Appearances, Ascension).

Sesson Purpose

By the end of this session participants will:

- Understand why the resurrection is essential.
- See how fear turns into mission.
- Recognize the significance of the ascension.
- Reflect on their role in the continuing story.

Opening Question (10 min.)

Ask:

- What changes when hope returns after loss?

Follow-up:

- Have you ever experienced a moment that completely reframed everything?

Transition:

- The resurrection doesn't merely comfort the disciples. It transforms them.

Burial: Silence and Finality (10 min.)

From the chapter "Joseph of Arimathea and Nicodemus give Jesus a hasty burial before sundown":

Ask:

- Why emphasize burial?
- Why include respected leaders like Joseph and Nicodemus?

Discuss:

- Burial confirms death.
- Hope appears sealed behind stone.

Reflection:

- God often works in the silence between promise and fulfillment.

The Empty Tomb: Shock and Confusion (15 min.)

From the chapter "The tomb is opened, and people can't find Jesus' body":

Ask:

- Why confusion before celebration?
- Why is the resurrection not immediately understood?

Discuss:

- The empty tomb creates questions.
- It demands explanation.

Reflection:

- Resurrection was not anticipated—even by believers.

The Emmaus Road: Recognition (15 min.)

From the chapter "Jesus appears to two of his followers on the way to Emmaus":

Ask:

- Why did Jesus walk with them without immediate revelation?
- What changes when they recognize him?

Discuss how recognition comes:

- Through Scripture.
- Through breaking bread.
- Through reflection.

Reflection:

- Sometimes Jesus is present before we perceive him.

Appearing to the Disciples: Fear to Courage (15 min.)

From the chapter "Jesus appears to his disciples for the first time":

Discuss before the resurrection:

- Hiding.
- Fear.
- Regret.

After resurrection:

- Boldness.
- Clarity.
- Mission.

Ask:

- What makes the difference?

Reflection on what the resurrection validates:

- His claims.
- His sacrifice.
- His authority.

Without resurrection, the cross is tragedy.
With resurrection, the cross is triumph.

The Ascension: A New Phase (15 min.)

From the chapter "The disciples watch Jesus ascend into the clouds":

Ask:

- Why not remain physically?
- What does ascension signify?

Discuss what ascension means:

- His work is complete.
- His authority is universal.
- The mission continues through his followers.

Reflection:

- The story doesn't end with disappearance.
  It begins with commissioning.

What Changes Because He Lives (10 min.)

Ask the group:

- What changes because of the resurrection?

Possible answers:

- Death loses finality.
- Fear loses power.
- Guilt loses control.
- Hope becomes permanent.
- Mission becomes urgent.

Discuss:

- Resurrection isn't symbolic encouragement.
  It's historical victory.

Group Discussion Questions (20 min.)

- Why is resurrection essential to Christian faith?
- What strikes you most about the Emmaus story?
- Why do the disciples move from fear to boldness?
- What does ascension communicate about Jesus' authority?
- If Jesus really lives, what must change in us?

Encourage thoughtful engagement.

Personal Application (10 min.)

Invite reflection:

- Where do I still live as if the tomb is sealed?
- How does resurrection reshape my fear?
- What mission has God entrusted to me?

Pray together.

Closing Thought

At the beginning of this journey, we saw:
"The Word became human and lived among his own people."

Now, we see:

- The Word risen.
- The Lamb victorious.
- The King ascended.

The story that began before creation now moves through us.

The resurrection isn't merely something to believe.

It's something to live.

Because he lives, we go.

CLOSING CELEBRATION SESSION: From Eyewitness to Witness

Purpose: To reflect on the journey, celebrate growth, reaffirm identity in Christ, and commission participants into ongoing discipleship.

Suggested Length: 75–90 minutes.

Session Goals

By the end of this session participants will:

- Recognize how their understanding of Jesus has deepened.
- Celebrate transformation and insight.
- Reaffirm their allegiance to Christ.
- Embrace their role in the continuing story.

Welcome and Gratitude (10 min.)

Open with warmth and gratitude.

Say something like:

For twelve sessions, we have walked chronologically through the life of Christ—from eternity past to ascension. We have seen joy, conflict, miracles, rejection, suffering, resurrection, and glory.

Today isn't just a conclusion.

It's a commissioning.

Return to Week One (15 min.)

In the introductory session, participants wrote one sentence answering:

Who is Jesus?

Invite everyone to take out that original sentence (or rewrite from memory if needed).

Now, ask them to write a new sentence:

- Who is Jesus to me now?

Allow quiet reflection.

Then invite volunteers to share.

Listen for differences:

- From "teacher" to "King."
- From "Savior" to "Sovereign."
- From "historical figure" to "living Lord."

Discuss briefly:

- What changed?
- What surprised you most in this study?

The Arc of the Story (15 min.)

Walk briefly through the five movements of the book:

- Incarnation — "The Word became human…"
- Authority — Storms stilled, demons expelled.
- Teaching — Kingdom ethics redefined.
- Cross — The Lamb offered.
- Resurrection and Ascension — The King enthroned.

Ask:

- Which movement impacted you most?
- Where did you feel conviction?

- Where did you feel comfort?

Personal Testimonies (15–20 min.)

Invite 3–5 volunteers to share briefly:

- One insight they gained.
- One way they changed.
- One challenge they are carrying forward.

Encourage authenticity over polish.

Remind them:

- Eyewitness accounts change history.
- Your witness changes lives.

Communion or Symbolic Response (optional – 15 min.)

If appropriate, conclude with communion.

Remind the group:

- At the Last Supper, Jesus reframed Passover around himself.
- The cross was not an accident.
- The resurrection was not a metaphor.
- The ascension was not an ending.

Take communion reverently, connecting it to the full narrative you have walked through.

If communion isn't possible, consider:

- Lighting candles (symbolizing light overcoming darkness).
- Writing a prayer of surrender.
- Standing together in a prayer of commitment.

From Eyewitness to Witness (10 min.)

Say:

- The original disciples were eyewitnesses.
- We are not eyewitnesses.
- But we are witnesses.

From the chapter "The disciples watch Jesus ascend into the clouds":

- He ascends.
- They remain.
- The mission continues.

Ask:

- Where is God sending you?
- Who needs to hear your story?
- What part of Christ's life do you feel called to reflect most clearly?

Group Declaration (5 min.)

Invite the group to stand (if appropriate) and read together:

We believe…

- Jesus is Lord.
- He lived.
- He died.
- He rose.
- He reigns.

And we follow him.

Final Reflection Questions

Discuss briefly:

- What habit from this study do you want to continue?
- How can you keep Scripture central?
- What does obedience look like this week?

Closing Prayer of Commission

Lord Jesus,

We have walked with you through joy and suffering, through teaching and triumph.

You are not only the Word who became flesh.

You are the risen King.

Send us now as faithful witnesses.

May we reflect your mercy, your courage, your truth, and your love.

In your name.

Amen.

Final Thought

This journey began with:

"In the beginning…"

It ends with ascension.

But the story is still being written—

In us.

www.ingramcontent.com/pod-product-compliance
Lightning Source LLC
LaVergne TN
LVHW020709110826
845149LV00012B/2172

* 9 7 8 1 9 6 2 8 4 8 4 3 5 *